WENSLEY CLARKSON

LEGAL HIGHS

Inside Secrets of the World's Newest and Deadliest Drugs

Quercus

First published in Great Britain in 2015 by Quercus Editions Limited

This paperback edition published in 2016 by

Quercus Editions Limited
Carmelite House
50 Victoria Embankment
London EC4Y 0DZ

An Hachette UK company

A CIP catalogue record for this book is available
from the British Library

PB ISBN 978 1 84866 716 7
EBOOK ISBN 978 1 84866 715 0

10 9 8 7 6 5 4 3 2 1

Typeset by Jouve (UK), Milton Keynes

Printed and bound in Great Britain by Clays Ltd, St Ives plc

To the innocent people who've lost their lives taking legal highs

CONTENTS

PART ONE

INVENTORS/CHEMISTS/PRODUCERS/BACKERS – ISRAEL, CHINA, ROMANIA, USA, UK, GERMANY, THAILAND

PART TWO
HANDLERS/RETAILERS/DEALERS – UK, USA, SOUTH AFRICA, JAPAN

PART THREE
TRANSPORTERS/DEALERS – USA, SPAIN, UK, HOLLAND

PART FOUR
TESTERS/DEALERS/PRISONS/CONSUMERS – UK, SOUTH AFRICA, SPAIN, SCANDINAVIA

PROLOGUE

The reality is we're chasing the chemists. There are people elsewhere in the world who're busy creating drugs, which mimic illegal drugs but are designed to be just outside the legal controls, in order to produce a product which is temporarily legal until we ban it.

John Corkery, co-author of a report on
UK deaths linked to legal highs

PURSAT, 170KM WEST OF PHNOM PENH, JUNE 2008

In the stifling heat of the south-west Cambodian jungle, several boys on scooters waited by the edge of a dirt track that was so overgrown with thick foliage it looked as if it was almost about to be swallowed up by the forest itself. They could hear the thundering sound of trucks approaching in the distance.

Eventually the noise grew louder as the trucks struggled

through the soupy tropical murk and grew ever closer to where the boys were sitting. The vehicles seemed to complain aloud as they negotiated the pandemonium of obstacles thrown in their path: potholes; rotting bridges; cascading foliage and shallow but lethal streams. Through the trees, the scooter boys spied the first of the trucks as it surged through pools of muddy water towards the village. But the trucks didn't bother to slow down through the village and even ignored a blood-red landmine marker hacked into a tree trunk.

Two hours later, the locals watched as the distant flames leapt so high they seemed to be almost singeing the dense grey clouds hanging over the nearby Cardamom Mountains. The trees crackled painfully as the fire seared through their thick bark.

But everyone knew why the trucks were there. The production of sassafras oil was destroying other types of trees, the livelihoods of many of those same local inhabitants and wreaking untold ecological damage on the environment. Of perhaps more importance though, is that sassafras oil is the essential ingredient in the world's most popular party drug, Ecstasy. So a decision had been made by the Cambodian government and their Australian counterparts to finally take action.

Those same flames shooting high into the sky eventually turned into putrid blue smoke as the sassafras oil cooked. Cambodian and Australian police donned masks to prevent the poisonous fumes from affecting them as they continued their 'slash and burn' operation.

In all they would eventually also destroy eighteen so-called ecstasy laboratories set up in this isolated jungle area to turn sassafras oil into what some people call 'the devil's candy'. Those labs had been heavily guarded until just a few days earlier when word reached the gangsters that the authorities were planning a raid.

The poorly paid workers who distilled the oil were said to be living on wildlife in the area as well as poaching rare species of animals for commercial gain. These included tigers, pangolins, peacocks, pythons and wild cats.

The burning oil, collected over weeks and months, had been distilled from the roots of the mreah prew phnom tree in laboratories that produced an average of 60 litres a day. That raid by the authorities destroyed in total 30 tons of safrole. If it had got to Holland, it could have been synthesized into 245 million doses of Ecstasy with a street value of US$7 billion. Instead, it was burnt to a cinder. The raid immediately had a profound and lasting impact on the worldwide trade in Ecstasy, but it also had a number of inadvertent consequences that the authorities could never have predicted.

Faced with such a catastrophic breakdown in their supply chain, the smugglers and dealers who had the clubbing scene sewn up were forced to invest vast sums of money into finding an alternative to traditional MDMA, or Ecstasy as it is better known. Soon the drug gangsters were flooding the marketplace with piperazines – chemical compounds that mimicked the effect of Ecstasy.

These were developed from substances used in the production of a number of medicines, such as worming treatment for animals, or compounds designed to induce migraines in medical research. Their effects were powerful, but ill defined. However, they were cheap and were a perfect substitute for Ecstasy following the raids in Cambodia. More importantly, they had a significant advantage over the product they had superseded: they were legal.

Welcome to the shadowy world of legal highs.

INTRODUCTION

While new harmful substances have been emerging with unfailing regularity on the drug scene, the international drug control system is floundering for the first time, under the speed and creativity of the phenomenon.

United Nations' *World Drug Report*

New psychoactive substances (NPS), dubbed 'legal highs', have come to blight countries across the globe. Their growing popularity means that in the new world order created by these synthesized narcotics, laboratories in Shanghai, Delhi and Tel Aviv are replacing the jungles of Central America and the opium fields of Afghanistan as the major battlegrounds on which the global war on drugs is being fought.

'Legal highs' are substances that produce similar effects to illegal drugs (such as cocaine, cannabis and Ecstasy) but are not controlled under existing anti-drug laws. These newly developed substances are not instantly outlawed by the authorities because there is not enough research about them to base a decision on. They have different chemical formulas to those officially banned under each nation's own carefully formulated version of the UK's Misuse of Drugs Act. The sheer volume of these drugs on the market makes it a logistical nightmare to monitor them. Many are developed so fast that there is little awareness of them when they become available.

By the middle of 2014, it was reckoned that tens of millions of pounds' worth of legal highs were being manufactured and then sold to users every month. Laboratories and factories in China, Europe and the US now provide the chemicals on an unprecedented scale, producing hundreds of tons of the compounds and selling the majority over the Internet. This exponential growth has attracted the attention of international drug cartels, whose experience, skills and contacts in respect of trafficking traditional drugs such as heroin and cocaine makes it easy for them to take advantage of this new and lucrative market.

In Scotland, Detective Chief Superintendent John Cuddihy, head of organized crime and counter-terrorism at Police Scotland, said: 'We are seeing a shift. Organized crime is now involved in the manufacture of these substances. They import the chemical constituents and then manufacture products that mimic cocaine or certain other drugs. In any business, you look to maximize profit and cut out the middle man.'

There is already clear evidence that crime syndicates are

secretly financing the making of their own brands of deadly synthetic psychoactives. Many of these characters are old-school gangsters angry that the traditional market in illegal drugs has been depleted by legal highs, so they've taken the law into their own hands. As one of my oldest underworld contacts 'Paddy' explained: 'Why shouldn't villains get a slice of this market? Who says we can't sell this stuff? We sat back and watched for years as all these legal highs swamped our market and now we're after a big piece of that business.'

On the other side of the law, police cite numerous recent high-profile deaths to new psychoactive substances as the driving force behind their attempts to control this illicit market for so-called legal highs. The most notorious of all these new designer drugs is mephedrone, also known as MCAT, Meow Meow, Drone, Meth, Mcat, Moonshine and Bubble. In many ways, the short history of mephedrone is emblematic of the journey taken by all legal highs.

Mephedrone was actually first synthesized in 1929, but remained hidden in obscurity until it was rediscovered in 2003. Originally produced in China, by 2007 it was widely available both over the Internet and over the counter. It was soon linked to numerous deaths and as early as 2008 the law enforcement agencies were already taking a close interest in its malign influence. The mephedrone phenomenon sparked the first full investigation by the authorities into the potency of legal highs. It was made illegal in most countries across the world in 2010. (In the UK, possession of mephedrone now carries a maximum sentence of five years' imprisonment, while dealers can receive up to fourteen years.) But that two-year window was enough time for mephedrone to establish itself as the drug of choice for many regular consumers of narcotics. By the time mephedrone was banned in the US and UK, it had become the fourth most popular drug on the planet, after marijuana, cocaine and Ecstasy.

Mephedrone is a compound of the amphetamine and cathinone classes. It bears a striking chemical resemblance to the cathinone compounds found in the khat plant of eastern Africa. Mephedrone is usually consumed in the form of tablets or a powder, which users can swallow, snort or inject, producing similar effects to MDMA, amphetamines and cocaine. Mephedrone produces euphoria, alertness, talkativeness and feelings of empathy. It's believed by many to enhance sensation during sex, and some vendors have even explicitly marketed it as a sexual stimulant.

But users say there is a substantial downside to taking this drug. According to joint research by the European Monitoring Centre for Drugs and Drug Addiction and Interpol, mephedrone has been 'found to have some of the same toxic features as MDMA [Ecstasy] and cocaine, causing acute problems similar to those seen with the use of illicit stimulants.' It can provoke anxiety and paranoia, heart palpitations and fits or seizures. Severe nosebleeds have also been reported after snorting.

There are numerous horror stories about the experiences of users. One teenager in central England started using mephedrone when he was offered it at a party. His mother later explained how he became completely addicted, aggressive and wired – staying up for days at a time before crashing and refusing to get out of bed. He lost his part-time job and was kicked out of school. After one heated confrontation over Christmas, the mother kicked her son out of the house. 'It had a massive, big effect on the family. I had a nervous breakdown,' the mother said. 'It was like my son couldn't live without it.'

Paul Bunt, from Avon and Somerset Police's Drug Expert Action Team, explained: 'Because mephedrone used to be a "legal high", people wrongly see it as harmless, it is anything but. It is highly addictive and its use is followed by very, very deep lows. In fact, we believe there is a link between mephedrone use and suicide. Other reported side-effects include fits, stomach, liver and heart problems and brain damage.'

The aftermath of the mephedrone phenomenon illustrated another characteristic of legal highs that shows just how difficult it is to police them. The authorities might be able to ban one substance, but they can be sure that if they do, there'll be another hundred new narcotics ready to take its place. Graeme Pearson, former head of the Scottish Drug Enforcement Agency, bemoaned the fact that Chinese drug labs manufacturing the next generation of psychotropics were effectively treating his country's teenagers as 'guinea pigs'. Pearson said that Far Eastern gangs were simply switching to the production of new drugs following the bans, with the intention of supplying the untested substances to those dealing in legal highs throughout the UK.

He added: 'Obviously the use of mephedrone is very dangerous, especially for young people, and it also proves problematic as we don't fully understand the substance's long-term effects. There is no doubt, people in these labs in China will already be manufacturing the next generation of non-illegal substances.'

That's not to say mephedrone has disappeared – it's perhaps truer to say that it's just found a new marketplace. Its criminalization drove it underground and also undoubtedly created even more demand for it than when it was legal. In the UK city of Liverpool, the banning of mephedrone sparked an increase in the price of the drug itself and made it even more popular. And the invasion of legal highs onto our streets has brought many other deadly consequences in their wake. Explained my underworld contact Paddy: 'The outlawing of certain legal highs actually plays right into our hands because it takes all the business away from the so-called "straight" sources such as head shops and websites and allows old-fashioned villains like me to move in and take over the market.'

In the aftermath of the mephedrone explosion, the rise of legal highs has become inexorable in every corner of the globe. Europe has surged to the forefront of the worldwide trade in legal highs with many hundreds of new brands coming onto the market in recent years. Online stores offering legal highs have been mushrooming in Europe: from

INTRODUCTION

170 in January 2010 to almost 1,000 by the summer of 2014. They offer a variety of substances and market them with exotic names such as 'Clockwork Orange', 'A3A', 'Blue Cheese', 'EM2 chiller', 'Go-Caine', or 'Benzo Fury'. Website sellers usually publish a disclaimer on their websites saying that if you use their products 'improperly' they will not be responsible for any consequences.

Almost 90 per cent of countries surveyed for the 2013 UN World Drugs Report attributed synthetic drugs a significant market share in the worldwide drugs arena. In the United States in 2013, 11 per cent of 17–18-year-olds admitted to using legal highs, and they are now the second most popular class of recreational drug among American students after cannabis. According to Linda Nilsson, project manager at the Sweden-based World Federation Against Drugs, figures for the Swedish market show that legal highs account for a significant segment of that nation's drug market, and while cannabis is still the most sold and consumed drug, 'numbers point towards this to be number two'. The lower prices and increased availability of legal highs compared with more traditional narcotics has undoubtedly attracted new consumers.

My underworld contact Paddy also told me about another significant reason that has contributed to the underworld's invasion of the market in legal highs. He said: 'The purity of stuff like coke and E has fallen so people have been switching to the legal highs in the hope of getting more "bangs for their bucks". I know a couple of gangs who actually cut their cocaine with legal-high substances to stretch out the product and increase the profit margins. That then turns off the punters, so they switch to legal highs in the hope they might work better.'

Paddy and other UK criminals openly admit to directly importing ingredients for products such as mephedrone as well as many of the substances used to create numerous other legal highs. They produce a vast range of pills and powders at secret factories, often set up in temporary barns or warehouses in isolated areas of the UK.

The majority of these chemical ingredients are imported from India, China and the Baltic States. Because most of them are not yet subject to the same draconian legislation as traditional narcotics, traffickers know that at worst they'll be charged under legislation covering the importation of medicine. Many gangsters are convinced manufacturing poses fewer risks, because they're importing legal substances, or sourcing them from the domestic market and law enforcement often shows little interest in monitoring such activities compared with smuggling illegal drugs. However, police insist they have woken up to this menace by stepping up their attempts to gather intelligence about both the products needed to make synthetic drugs and the kind of people who have the right kind of knowledge to 'process' the ingredients. Police believe they have the right to arrest these legal-high gangsters on the basis they're responsible for the death or injury of anyone who deliberately or inadvertently takes such substances that they have provided.

INTRODUCTION

As one expert has pointed out: 'Although these drugs are marketed as legal substances, this does not mean that they're safe or approved for people to use. Some drugs marketed as legal highs actually contain some ingredients that are illegal to possess.'

But so far the number of arrests has been low compared to the figures relating to the 'traditional' illegal drugs.

Many of the new breed of drug bosses keep their activities low-key by using legitimate front businesses to hide their drug activities. In the West of England, one crime syndicate uses the production of manure and compost as a cover for manufacturing legal highs. 'It's a perfect cover because many of the ingredients needed are identical,' explained Paddy. 'These legal highs are a dream come true for old-school villains like me. None of the risk and a much bigger profit. You can't get much better than that.'

Back in Scotland, Detective Chief Superintendent John Cuddihy added: 'We are certainly seeing a number of organized crime groups diversifying into this. They are manufacturing wherever they can find a facility to host it, wherever they can covertly carry out business. They need somewhere where they can hide their nefarious business from others, where they can bring in bulk ingredients.'

Many governments have tried to push through reclassification of drugs laws in a bid to stamp out the legal highs but the wheels of justice roll very slowly. 'No country can issue new laws left, right and centre. It takes time and that plays right into the hands of the legal-high gangsters,' explained one expert. In the UK, a special unit has been set up to monitor, identify and then tackle the supply of new psychoactive substances threatening public health. But it is a glacial process that in many instances cannot keep up with the new drugs coming on the market. At least 600 chemicals are listed by name in the UK's Misuse of Drugs Act. But since 2010, the UK government has managed to ban only fifteen.

Some nations are so slow to outlaw certain drugs that they provide a legal location to produce the substances, many of which are then sold on the Internet. In other words, these legal-high dealers cannot be touched by law enforcement even if they're selling such drugs to countries that have banned these substances.

No wonder so many legal highs are produced by legitimate-sounding companies headquartered in undeveloped countries who encourage new businesses to improve their own home economy, irrelevant of the nature of these companies. This means cheaper start-up costs compared to production in the Western World.

According to the Monitoring Centre for Drugs and Drug Addiction, European organized crime groups 'produce synthetics cheaply in Africa and Asia and distribute their products to markets in Europe.' China, India and Thailand provide many of the substances used in the conversion process. But West, North and East Africa are expected to become increasingly attractive locations to producers of legal highs due to improved transport links with profitable markets in Europe, new local market opportunities and inexpensive labour. Linda Nilsson said that Swedish Customs officials believe most synthetic cannabinoids come from inside Europe while synthetic cathinones come from China and India.

To make matters worse, chemists as far away as China and India don't just sit back and wait for their products to be made illegal. Often they've already created the next variation of a substance and have it ready to hit the streets before the ink on the banning order of its parent drug has dried. One renowned UK scientist heads up a lab where 29,000 different drugs have been tested. He says twenty years ago it was a huge deal discovering a new drug, which would be followed by a celebration in the pub. These days they discover 'at least' fifty to seventy a year.

But perhaps the most worrying aspect of the criminal 'invasion' of the legal-high market is that unscrupulous gangsters often add unknown chemicals, manufactured in labs on the other side of the world, to drugs to bypass existing laws. Law enforcement agencies say these sorts of criminal manufacturing operations use cheap and toxic compounds to do this, something that has the additional benefit of boosting their profit margins. This doesn't necessarily guarantee their products will provide customers with the ultimate 'high', but it does substantially increase the risk of the drug causing potentially catastrophic side-effects. Many drugs sold as 'legal' have actually been found to contain at least one substance that is, in fact, illegal. According to a recent United Nations World Drug Report, many new synthetic substances come onto the market every year creating a confusing situation where many users are playing Russian roulette with their drug choices because there is no evidence to support claims that these new substances even work.

Producers of new legal highs constantly monitor the Internet for new developments via published medical studies and even geeky chatrooms in order to create new products. Yet most of these 'inventors' of legal highs have little or no chemical experience. As one expert said: 'That means they could be producing literally anything, which is pretty scary.' James Capra, US Drug Enforcement Agency chief of operations, said at a news conference in June, 2013: 'These so-called chemists are constantly tweaking the molecules and it changes the whole structure of the drug, so the drug becomes legal and we're at it again.'

The subtle changes in the formulas can also have lethal, highly toxic effects.

'Every time you alter that molecule, you could end up with a drug that is better or you could theoretically make a monster,' said Dr. Mark Ryan, director of the US's Louisiana Poison Center.

Most of these chemicals have never been tested for human consumption before, so there is no way of knowing if they are safe to ingest. That means users can never be certain what they're taking and what the effects might be. For instance, a whole slew of products sold as 'legal cannabis' might more accurately be described as a small amount of plant matter cut with a witch's brew of toxic chemicals that can cause everything from psychotic episodes to paranoia and even death. The US Substance Abuse and Mental Health Services Administration reported 28,531 emergency-department visits involving a synthetic cannabinoid during 2011, more than double the previous year. These substances have been linked with teens shooting themselves, athletes collapsing and dying and even the gruesome devouring of a family dog. Dr Mark Ryan added: 'You don't murder people high on marijuana. People who smoke marijuana end up at a convenience store buying a honeybun and a carton of orange juice.'

Experts say legal-high users are often being reduced to confused or even 'catatonic' states by what they've taken: 'These young people are being found in alleyways, getting knocked down and falling off heights. This is a particular danger for vulnerable young women.' One hospital doctor outlined some of the effects these new narcotics can have on your body: 'Typically, these drugs make you feel more energetic, your body temperature rises and you begin to feel agitated – it is a vicious cycle. You will be very hot to the touch and that is a danger sign. You could then collapse through lack of fluids or the heart can stop without warning. If you survive this bit, your muscles will cook themselves and break down, releasing protein into your bloodstream, which blocks the kidneys and causes them to fail. So you will end up on dialysis. The liver also gets damaged from the heat and some people end up with long-term liver failure.' Most weekends in large cities such as London, hospital staff are dealing with the direct effects of these legal-high drugs such as poisonings and falls, as well as the knock-on effects, which are often violence and assaults. As one medic said: 'I cannot stress how dangerous these drugs are. You can never be sure what you are taking and how it will affect your body. Don't take the risk.'

The other 'Russian Roulette' aspect of legal highs is that many users don't know what sort of dose they are supposed to take or what effect they can expect from the drug. They can't even be sure which drug they're using. Even when users think they've taken a named street drug, doctors often find those substances have been mixed with new toxins, which they don't have medical knowledge of. Medical staff in hospitals across the Western world report that they frequently attend to 'overdose' patients who don't know what they've taken, which means doctors often don't know exactly how to treat a patient. 'It's a bit of a nightmare scenario,' said one UK accident and emergency doctor. 'When a patient comes in with an overdose of a traditional drug such as cocaine or heroin we know how to deal with it, but it's impossible to treat people who've taken substances that we know nothing about.'

One doctor explained: 'We are treating the symptoms of these new drugs rather than being able to give direct treatment for the drug. I can run a drugs test on someone and it comes back clear. But I know this person has taken drugs.'

The same doctor said that there was increasing evidence that more people were consuming legal highs at house parties where they mix their drug intake and also drank to excess.

INTRODUCTION

He explained: 'There has been a shift from the so-called "clubbing" drug culture, where people might collapse in nightclubs, to teenagers and people in their twenties taking these drugs at house parties. This is an added danger because you don't have club staff looking out for their welfare. Also, people are more likely to drink or take drugs to excess or mix both in a private party environment.' As one expert said: 'Legal highs used alongside alcohol pose even greater risks to health and should be avoided. This is a tinderbox situation. You are literally taking your life into your own hands each time you take legal highs but to mix them with alcohol and other drugs could lead to even more fatal consequences.'

But despite the risks – and numerous high-profile deaths – hospital emergency departments throughout the UK and the US say the numbers gambling their lives on these drugs continue to rise.

It took my underworld contact Paddy to sum up the legal-high phenomenon. 'Criminals care about making money. They don't care about what it is they're selling. As long as there is a demand they will feed it. Is it really so surprising that legal highs have taken off in the way they have? I think not.'

AUTHOR'S NOTE

When I first began researching this book I presumed that because I was dealing with 'Legal Highs' rather than 'traditional' illegal drugs, people would be willing and open to talk about their involvement. Nothing could be further from the truth. The people who make their living from legal highs are even more secretive than many of the Colombian coke barons and Moroccan hash kings I've come across during thirty years as a true crime writer.

These legal-high 'businessmen' live in constant fear of being arrested on the basis that what they sell could be outlawed at any moment. It's a Catch-22. These substances are known as legal highs but they don't stay that way for long and that has helped create the underworld you are about to read about.

So I've had to explore this strange netherworld with great care and that makes the contributions in this book all the more revelatory. I've been allowed into the legal-high world despite the fears and trepidation of so many about being publicly exposed. As a result, many of the characters you are about to read about were given new identities to protect them from prosecution. But without them, this book would not have been possible.

Much of the dialogue used here was drawn from actual interviews, some from documentary sources, while a few descriptions were reconstituted from the memory of others. This book deliberately sets out to be a dark journey into the heart and soul of the legal-high drug trade. In it, I will delve into the background of how these drugs are created, how they end up available for public consumption and the effects these drugs produce as well as the shadowy criminal enterprises making fortunes from them. This book doesn't set out to be overly preachy – my overall intention is to provide a balanced view.

You'll meet a wide variety of characters, who all share an involvement in the legal high 'industry' worldwide. On the one hand are those people making money out of legal highs and watching on as many youngsters experiment with a wide range of different drugs that provide differing, and sometimes lethal effects. These are not sad individuals whose life has spiralled out of control thanks to drugs. No, these are dispassionate businessmen who are part of a vast global enterprise. Legal highs are set to overtake the sales of substances such as cocaine, heroin and cannabis within the next five years. Yet very few people over the age of thirty-five have any in-depth knowledge of this new development in narco-crime. 'It must have been like this in the early

AUTHOR'S NOTE

sixties when illegal drugs first made serious inroads into the world's youth,' says one expert. Today, only a minority of parents are fully aware of the dangers of legal highs and virtually none of them knows the names of any of the substances openly available on the Internet or in their friendly local head shop.

At the other end of the spectrum you'll meet the consumers; some are the sort of people who try different legal highs and then write about the effects online. Such consumers only do drugs 'for a treat', they claim. We'll encounter them in their normal environment as they purchase substances online. But it should never be forgotten they're still taking a huge risk as noted by the toxicologists featured in this book. After all, these drugs often clearly state on the packet that they are 'not for human consumption' and are distributed as 'research chemicals': the overriding message, however, is that legal doesn't mean safe. Yet that doesn't stop them being consumed by the bucketload.

Wensley Clarkson, 2015

LEGAL HIGHS THROUGH THE AGES

It was a day that will remain blazingly clear in my memory, and one which unquestionably confirmed the entire direction of my life. I understood that our entire universe is contained in the mind and the spirit. We may not choose to find access to it, we may even deny its existence, but it is indeed there inside us, and there are chemicals that can catalyse its availability.

Dr Alexander Shulgin, godfather of Ecstasy

In some ways, you could argue that the story of mankind is really just the story of our attempts to get high. Archaeologists recently uncovered a mix of betel-nut juice and quicklime spat out by a pioneer 'psychonaut' some 9,000 years before the birth of Christ. But we soon moved on to more powerful and sophisticated hallucinogenics.

It all really kicked off in the sixties, when anarchic 'hippies' with their Kool-Aid Acid Tests introduced thousands of people, with relative safety, to the delights and mind-expanding properties of good-quality LSD. As the Vietnam war dragged on into the seventies, underground chemists were involved in their own arms war, creating new psychoactive substances designed to get round existing narcotics legislation. This was how synthetic drugs came to be first properly developed.

Yet the key to the recent surge in the development of legal highs stems from both the pioneering research and the proselytizing fervour of one eccentric professor called Alexander Shulgin who invented, produced and then wrote about his 'narcotic discoveries', only for them to be spotted by an ever curious, yet unsuspecting, public.

This all began back in the so-called 'innocent' 1950s where, like many other intellectuals of the time, US-based Professor Shulgin tried mescaline – a natural and at that time legal hallucinogen present in certain cacti. He found the experience so transformative that he gave over the rest of his life to radical psychedelic research. He constantly tinkered with the molecules of drugs to produce new compounds that would have what he saw as 'novel and interesting effects'.

Shulgin's aim was to produce substances that could 'enlighten' the mind and which, ultimately, resulted in the birth of legal highs as we now know them. Shulgin carefully documented every step of his 'development work' and even tested many substances on himself, reporting every new breakthrough. At the time, Shulgin was working with a US government-approved licence, which enabled him to produce samples of outlawed drugs to help the US Drug Enforcement Agency, who needed to verify samples of drugs to compare them with substances they had seized. His wife, a psychotherapist, often used his chemicals with empathoid and aphrodisiac qualities for couples attending therapy and sexual dysfunction sessions.

The drug with which he has come to be most closely associated is methylenedioxymethamphetamine (MDMA), the principal component of Ecstasy. It was actually first synthesized by a German pharmaceutical firm in 1912 to get around a patent on a common clotting agent, and later used by the US military in experiments in mind control. In 1965 Shulgin got a tip-off from a fellow researcher about it and he began looking more closely at the components. On 12 September 1976, Shulgin successfully synthesized MDMA Ecstasy. He quickly shared his discovery with his friends. Like his wife, they worked in psychotherapy and recognized how they could use the drug's capacity to dismantle social barriers and personal inhibitions in their work.

The professor wrote up his research and published it in a book called *PiHKAL: A Chemical Love Story*. This tome was bought by hundreds of underground chemists and, before long, illegal production of this new drug had begun. This was aided by the fact that Shulgin's production techniques depended on chemicals that could be easily acquired by almost anyone. In the case of Ecstasy the key component was safrole, the essential oil produced by distilling the root bark of trees such as the ones already mentioned earlier in this book in Cambodia.

For almost thirty years, Shulgin invented a whole medicine cabinet's worth of psychotropics. The professor's other discoveries included drugs like DiPT, an analogue of a psychedelic chemical found in some plants and fungi. This was manipulated in order to produce the effect that it made anyone listening to music hear the sounds an octave or so lower than before. Shulgin insisted he was convinced by the positive benefits of cognitive enhancers. Even though he later admitted many of those chemical inventions had sparked disturbing effects he had never envisaged, he never once regretted his actions.

In 1994 the DEA – the same organization that Shulgin had once worked for – raided his laboratory in California. But they were only able to prove the master chemist had 'problematic' record keeping. Even if they had been able to secure a prosecution, it would have been too late: Shulgin's detailed research was by then already in the public domain and providing the readymade blueprint for Ecstasy as we know it.

MDMA was said to give users a euphoric, timeless sensation and it eventually found its way into the gay club scene in Texas in the mid-1980s. Soon celebrities in the US were linked to Ecstasy, giving it a glamorous reputation as the 'drug of choice' for party people. By 1988, MDMA had moved across the Atlantic to Europe where, in places as diverse as Ibiza, Manchester, London and beyond, it was a catalyst in the explosion of Acid House music. The up and coming rave scene's infatuation with Ecstasy and illegal warehouse parties was an uncanny echo of the first summer of love. By the time the first wave of Ecstasy use had passed, Shulgin's experiments had changed the minds of millions of young people and laid the ground for the invasion of a horde of exotic drugs that even he could never have dreamed up.

But it wasn't until the onset of the Internet in the late 1990s, that the work of Shulgin and other chemists was disseminated beyond a small network of scientists. The World Wide Web enabled anyone to access the key books and journals, many of which were written by Shulgin. These studies and research papers were soon promoted as instruction manuals, discussed and dissected online by thousands of amateur chemists, many of whom were keen to cash in on the MDMA craze.

At the same time, communities of self-styled 'psychonauts' began to appear – drug-users who hunted the Internet for firms selling legal drugs. They tried the fresh products out, and recorded their experiences – much like Shulgin did all those years ago – by swapping notes online. Millions of pages of discussion about the use and effects of a mind-bending range of these novel stimulants are now available to anyone browsing the web.

Before long the so-called 'King' of legal highs, mephedrone, emerged on the marketplace. It would later be joined by buphedrone, flephedrone, ethylone and butylone to name but a few.

Internet forums dedicated to selling and discussing mephedrone and other new legal highs proliferated. Websites were able to circumvent food and medicine laws by claiming, with a straight face, that their products were 'plant food'. Packaged in rave-style graphics and labelled with absurd instructions such as, 'Water your plants no more than once a week. Will make your garden bloom!', they didn't fool anyone. Another common way of dodging various laws was to brand the drugs as 'research chemicals'.

Initially, knowledge of the new synthetic narcotics was pretty much limited to these so-called psychonauts. Today though, it's become a huge global business. Tons of legal highs are delivered by post every year around the world. Forty thousand such parcels an hour pass through the international postal hub in Coventry in the UK. A handful of suspect parcels are held back for testing in the examination room and they almost always test positive for legal highs.

Today, police, pill-poppers and professors are facing a cornucopia of drug types so diverse it makes Procter & Gamble look like a local sweet shop. These psychoactives are very cheap, incredibly easy to buy, and, of course, legal.

The UK appears to be leading this disturbing trend. Since 2010, four times more new legal highs were found here than in any other European country. The UK also has the highest number of drug-related deaths per year (almost 3,000). In 2012 the English town of Swindon reported a record number of hospital admissions due to legal highs, while Glasgow has seen a mind-boggling 358 per cent increase in legal-high admissions over recent years.

A survey of more than 300 people across South London's gay and gay-friendly nightclubs in the summer of 2013 found two in three clubbers had tried legal highs. In 2012 a survey of 15,500 respondents (albeit the sample were regular clubbers rather than representative of the general UK population) revealed one in five had taken a legal high in the last year. It also showed that they no longer just purchased their legal highs online: buying them from shops, friends and from dealers.

With the growth in the popularity of these substances has come a corresponding notoriety. On any weekend, in clubs, pubs and bars across Britain and many other western countries, millions of young people will take legal highs. With luck – and it will take a lot of good fortune – virtually none of them will die horribly as a result. But what is certain is that many thousands will experience a bad trip that may ruin their health, and their lives, for ever.

Since the start of the last decade, the legal-high scene has had to absorb the fallout resulting from the tragic deaths of a number of users. In a series of unrelated but infamous incidents, three young American men overdosed on a compound named 2C-T-7 that had first been detailed in Shulgin's books. The resulting backlash against this and other early versions of legal highs was then compounded by high-profile busts conducted by a US/UK anti-drugs operation,

Operation Ismene. Police raided firms in the US and homes in Britain and arrested 22 people for buying that same designer hallucinogen, 2C-T-7, which had already been made illegal in the UK. However, few of the people arrested in these raids were actually involved in the manufacture and distribution of the drugs – most were simply customers. The psychonauts kept a low profile for a time afterwards, but this reticence was only temporary.

What law enforcement officers – and many others too – failed to understand was that the drug market would simply reappear in a different form. The industry surrounding the new narcotics was as complex and protean as the chemical compounds it was producing and selling. This was in large part because much of the action was playing out in the darker corners of the World Wide Web. The Internet dissolved borders, offered almost infinite flexibility and allowed those involved to retain a degree of anonymity and security that would never have been possible before. What I wanted to find out was, who are these people and how have they created a lucrative underworld filled with lethal legal highs?

PART ONE

INVENTORS/CHEMISTS/ PRODUCERS/BACKERS – ISRAEL, CHINA, ROMANIA, USA, UK, GERMANY, THAILAND

There's a misguided assumption that the guys running clandestine chemistry labs have bad complexions and wear plaid shirts and that they are slightly dim and just follow cookbook recipes. That's a mistake. These guys are incredibly bright. They are head-and-shoulders – intellectually, certainly – above some of the politicians who are attempting to legislate against them.

US legal-highs expert

In 2008 – following that slash and burn operation in Cambodia – the Internet fuelled the huge appetite for new legal-high products. The biggest names back then included substances such as Neo Doves and Sub Coca. These were produced by a firm in Israel that refused to reveal what was actually in them. Sold in capsules, users agreed unanimously that they worked, and said they felt like a cross between Ecstasy and cocaine. They were massively popular, despite the deep reservations some people retained about the mysterious ingredients of the new compound. Soon Neo Doves and Sub Coca were selling in their hundreds of thousands. It also became clear they were highly addictive, with users reporting they'd gone on crazed binges for days. It was music to the ears of the producers of these drugs. Others quickly decided to join the legal-high bandwagon.

Soon something akin to a chemical gold-rush began to emerge on the Internet, with dozens of new players popping up daily. The new drugs could be bought for around £1,000 to £2,500 per kilo and sold for £10,000 – and it was all legal.

At the same time another group of Israeli scientists began to try and grab some of this potentially lucrative global market for themselves by creating multiple legal highs. They insist to this day they did not make 'much money' from these products. But few believe them as conservative estimates of their earning potential are in the tens of millions of US dollars. Today some of those same Israeli scientists work full time to create new drugs similar to the components of popular illegal drugs. They claim testing does take place, first with the inventors themselves, followed by animals and lastly through human volunteers. But there is no doubt that the long-term effects of these drugs remain relatively unknown.

Israel's thriving legal-high underworld also fed a ravenous domestic demand from the nation's youth, especially in big cities such as Tel Aviv. The earliest legal high to emerge on the streets of Israel was Hagigat, which was quickly marketed as a party drug. The active ingredients of Hagigat – the word is a blend of the Hebrew word *hagiga* ('party') and *ghat* – were a combination of methamphetamine and cathine, a phenethylamine-type substance carefully isolated from the plant and then sold in capsules that could be swallowed or emptied out and the contents snorted.

It took some years before Hagigat was officially outlawed by the Israeli authorities. Dealers then simply began developing new versions based on different types of methamphetamine. Hagigat available today is very different to its predecessors. Dealers admit it now includes a wide range of fillers cut with the speed, including aspirin, lactose and even – according to Israeli authorities – cornflour.

But the really chilling element of the Hagigat trade emerged when it was discovered that many hardened drug addicts were using it intravenously in south Tel Aviv. These were users – often young and homeless with severe addiction problems – who either didn't have enough money to buy heroin or wanted to be able to shoot up in peace without being arrested. It is widely believed that intravenous use of the drug has sparked a sharp rise in HIV infection in Tel Aviv. In 2012 an outbreak of hepatitis A that caused 69 cases as opposed to only seven the previous year helped support these claims.

More lethal still is the Hagigat sold south of Tel Aviv's Menachem Begin Street, which is designed to be more easily soluble in water and thus simpler to inject. In and around the city's bus station, abandoned syringes provided ample evidence of this apparent epidemic. However, in the richer suburbs of Tel Aviv, Hagigat remained largely a party drug used mainly by middle-class teenagers.

Today in Tel Aviv, the 'businessmen' selling legal highs insist they're not involved in the Hagigat trade. They claim their substances are 'much classier' and that they form part of a lucrative export business making tens of millions of US dollars each year.

CHAPTER 1

AVI

As the early sun rises between the skyscrapers of downtown Tel Aviv, London-born Avi, forty-six, is stuck in morning rush-hour traffic as he heads to his laboratory on the edge of the city. Avi has a masters in biochemistry from one of London's most prestigious universities. He has a wife and two kids back at his penthouse apartment and his job description of 'research executive' gives no clue as to his role in creating some of the most potent legal highs in the world.

Avi's much more infamous contemporary is a notorious character known as Dr Zee, a mysterious Israeli-born mathematician hailed as the man behind mephedrone and many other legal highs. Avi considers himself to be just as much of a player as Zee and that may well have been why he allowed me to interview him about his top-secret drug storage facility. He even explained how easy it was to get around the Misuse of Drugs Act – a new chemical bond here, a different

7

element there. It was shocking how straightforward it all sounded.

Avi revealed how his own experimentation with drugs in the late 1990s in London helped turn him from a poorly paid researcher into an immensely successful producer of legal highs. At his laboratory he talked about the way he researched and created these substances and why he felt no guilt about the lack of safety checks surrounding so many of them, which are easily available on the Internet.

After chatting for an hour, Avi took me into his 'control tower' where a team of three young scientists were busy 'cooking' Avi's next ingenious pharmaceutical invention. But this was no scene from *Breaking Bad* with a rundown campervan doubling for a lab. The laboratory was spotlessly clean, filled with modern equipment and Avi's 'staff' were even clothed in immaculate starched white clothing.

'This is my centre of operations,' said Avi, proudly. 'I'm a bit like one of those mad scientists you see on the old movies. I tweak, mix and cook all day. It's fun. Oh, hang on, that makes me sound more like Walter White from *Breaking Bad* but I'm sure you know what I mean.'

Avi keeps his identity secret because he knows better than anyone that many of his concoctions will be outlawed by governments within months, if not weeks of their introduction into the lucrative marketplace. He's been warned at least half a dozen times by Israeli law enforcement officials that he is being closely monitored.

'It's all like a game of bluff in a sense,' he says. 'I put

together a new product but I always make sure it is easy to tweak it so that once it is made illegal I can produce another version that does not break the law. Sure, there are many people here in Israel who would like to see me in jail but I am doing nothing wrong in the eyes of the law. They cannot touch me but I am very careful not to push my luck.'

Avi admitted he spent more time and money producing these hybrid versions of various existing substances than actually developing entirely new legal highs. 'It's just the way this business goes. You have to build in all sorts of expenses to cover the "game" as I like to call it. I experiment a lot. After all, I am a scientist. I enjoy learning new things and that happens virtually every day in this job.'

Avi admitted the most vulnerable aspect of his job were the cat and mouse games he has to play with the authorities to ensure he manages to stay one step ahead of every fresh clampdown on legal highs. He moves his laboratory on the outskirts of Tel Aviv regularly because he believes the local police are under immense pressure from authorities inside and outside Israel to crack down on the trade in these synthetic narcotics. 'One cop I know says they all think they have better things to do than chase guys like me.'

Avi continued: 'Hey, they call this stuff legal highs but I'm made to feel like a criminal for producing the stuff. I often tell the police that as far as I'm concerned I'm doing nothing wrong. But I recognize that the police and other authorities are under immense pressure from countries like the UK and US to shut people like me down so I respect that by moving labs every six to nine months, so that the wrong people never get to hear about where I am operating. I don't want to rub their noses in it because otherwise my business will sink and I'll end up in jail.'

Avi's interest in synthetic drugs first emerged when he was a student in London and attended raves in the early-to-mid-nineties. 'The rave scene was something else, man, I tell you. I was just a country boy from the Middle East and suddenly I found myself immersed in this crazy party scene. Sure, I took lots of Ecstasy and to begin with I loved the stuff. It made me feel so free and uninhibited. Everyone at my college took it at weekends. But then one time I had a strange experience with a different batch of Ecstasy. I felt very sick and it really bugged me that it was so different from the early stuff, so I dissected the ingredients of one of those tabs of bad E that had been sold to me in a club.

'Well, I was stunned to discover that it contained nothing more than a few basic ingredients, most of which I could have mixed together in a small lab. That's when I started experimenting with my own "recipes". I was encouraged by some of my college friends because they trusted me a lot more than the local drug dealer!'

Avi confessed that for the last year of his stay in London, he spent much of his time concocting his own unique versions of Ecstasy. 'I'm a curious sort of fellow and I wanted to develop the perfect Ecstasy tablet. But I also wanted to make sure its ingredients were safe for human consumption.'

Initially, admitted Avi, his experimentation was a 'complete fucking disaster'. He explained: 'It's a learning process like everything else. At first I couldn't get the mix right because you have to be very careful not to overdose the ingredients, otherwise people get sick and the effects are too extreme. But I am a very patient guy and I stuck at it because I knew there was a big market out there if I could produce the perfect product.'

Avi insisted he never once encouraged anyone to take any of his early attempts at Ecstasy tablets in London 'until I'd tested it out on myself'. He went on: 'I can tell you, I had a few bad trips while testing out my Ecstasy but I felt I had to be the one to be the guinea pig. It wasn't fair to expect my friends to take the risks when I was the one who'd created the stuff in the first place.'

Avi recalled that for almost a year in London, he struggled to 'come up with the perfect Ecstasy tab.' He explained: 'Either it was too weak or too strong. Then one day I took yet another sample and this time it worked like a dream – literally. The Ecstasy kicked in gently and gave me an overwhelmingly happy feeling, but it wasn't too strong and uncontrollable. I was still in control of myself and confident and content. But to everyone else I was acting completely normal. That's what a good E tab should do for you.'

Within months, explained Avi, he'd set up his own laboratory in a rented flat in north London and was selling 100 Ecstasy tablets a day. 'It took me about an hour for each

11

batch. I had it all down to a fine art. I sold the tablets for £10 each and, if you do the math, you can see that it was a highly profitable little business.'

By this time, Avi had already made some big career choices. 'I had my science degree but I didn't want to end up being a Mr Nobody working my socks off in a giant lab in the US, producing new versions of cattle feed or whatever. It just didn't appeal to me.

'I'd got a taste of what it was like to be a chemical entrepreneur and I liked it a lot. I liked being my own boss too. But the trouble was that it was fine to pump out party pills from a student's apartment but if I was going to make a career of it I needed to get serious. I also knew that staying in London was asking for trouble, so I decided to head back home to Israel.'

It was, admitted Avi, a risky strategy. 'Israel at that time was very anti-drugs. The police cracked down hard on cocaine and cannabis users and to a certain extent they had been much more successful than most countries at eradicating excessive drug taking thanks to the tight security at our borders. Exporting stuff out of Israel is another matter. That's easy. I also knew there was a massive market of bored kids in Israel who would love to be turned on to stuff like E. It was a marketplace waiting to be exploited but I had to be very secretive at first.'

That's when Avi came up with what he calls his 'business brainwave'. 'It suddenly dawned on me that I didn't even need to break the law by producing my own version of

Ecstasy. I tried to explain all this to my parents and their friends because I was so naive I thought some of them might invest in my idea. But they couldn't see the difference between illegal highs and something that was completely one hundred per cent legal. It was all drugs to them and they hated the stuff!

'But I decided to go out on my own. I pulled apart all the ingredients that I'd been using back in London for my home-produced pills and replaced certain ingredients with herbal extracts and readily available substances that could be easily bought across the counter in any big hardware store.'

And so Avi's career in legal highs took off. 'It was about ten years ago that I started a serious production line. Just like back in London, I used myself as the guinea pig and then allowed my closest friends to sample my produce. But the big difference was that I could sell the stuff on the open market, just so long as I disguised it a bit, of course.'

Avi's concoctions used everyday substances but, he explained, combined together they produced out of the ordinary results. 'One of my closest and oldest friends was a lawyer and he advised me on the best way to package up the products. He pointed out that nothing I was producing had been given the same level of testing as, say, regular pharmaceuticals so I had to get around this very carefully otherwise my whole operation would be quickly shut down.

'That's when I realized the best way to deal with such logistical problems was to be one hundred per cent honest.

Let me explain: I was using all these everyday substances to concoct my produce, so my lawyer friend said why not simply call them by their original name and then no one can accuse you of deceiving them in any way. It was so logical but it was something I'd never thought of before.'

And, says Avi, there was another label that needed to be put on every container. 'My lawyer friend said to make sure it said not for human consumption, then it would be impossible for me to be sued or arrested. It got round all the rules and regulations when it comes to anything that is consumed by people.'

Once he'd got the wording right on his packaging, Avi says his products 'began to fly off the shelves'. He explained: 'I made sure I never called them legal highs because I knew that might make it easier for the police to come after me. The phrase legal highs was coined by someone else but it did me a big favour because it helped the youngsters not to be afraid of what it was I was producing.'

Initially, Avi's legal-high products were sold through record shops and from kiosks in the big cities such as Tel Aviv and Jerusalem. 'They were selling in big numbers but of course that's when my first problems began because the parents of many teenagers were not happy. They wanted my stuff banned but then they found out that was impossible because there was nothing illegal about them.'

Avi insisted that he has 'never knowingly broken the law' but admitted he learned not to discuss his 'profession' outside a tightly knit circle of friends. 'It wasn't just the authorities that I encountered. Word of my products got to the Tel Aviv underworld and I soon heard that some very heavy characters were asking around about who I was.'

Avi claims that sales of his legal highs gradually outstripped the cocaine and cannabis being peddled by traditional drug dealers. 'That's when I started to get a bit freaked out because I knew the criminals would come calling one day. My family got a visit from a heavy-looking guy one day, who said he needed to talk to me. I don't know to this day how he managed to get my name but it scared the shit out of me and my family.

'I discovered that not only were the gangsters angry about the way my products were affecting their illicit drug business, but they were planning to force me to produce new products for them. Well, I can tell you that was the last thing I wanted! One of the great things about my business was that I was my own boss and no one made me do anything I didn't want to do. The idea of a bunch of evil criminals giving me orders and no doubt ripping me off did not appeal to me at all.'

Everything came to a head for Avi when the leader of a notorious gang of drug barons based in Tel Aviv sent a message to him via a local police officer. 'Can you believe it? This gangster had the cops in his pocket and he sent a threatening message to me via his favourite crooked detective! I was told that I would have to double my output and in exchange the criminals would leave me and my family alone. Well, this was a very tricky situation because I knew perfectly well that once I started working for the criminals there would be no going back. I would be like putty in their hands and they would also steal all my profits.'

So Avi set up a meeting with the Tel Aviv gangsters. He explained: 'I'm a pragmatic sort of guy and I reckoned that going into the lion's den was the only way to properly deal with such a problem.' He continued: 'I made sure we met in a public place so they couldn't hold any guns to my head and we ended up meeting in the parking lot of a McDonald's. Not very original but it summed up the sort of people I was dealing with. The main guy was very friendly but there was this underlying threat all the time that if I did not co-operate then something "might happen" to my friends and family.

'I was very cool with this guy. I didn't fight with him but then he made a point of showing me he was armed, so there wouldn't have been much point! At the end of the meeting in the back of his limo, I asked for a bit of time to decide whether I would go into business with him. This guy must have thought I was like putty in his hands because he just nodded his head at me when I asked for time and then said, "You got twenty-four hours."

'Well, I knew that if I was going to do anything it had better be quick because otherwise this guy was going to own me and my legal-high business and maybe even kill me if I didn't do what he asked. So I went straight to one of my best friends, a reporter on the local TV news and produced secret filming footage from my meeting with the criminal. You see, that guy had completely underestimated me because I had recorded every word of our meeting in that parking lot with a secret camera hidden in my key ring.

'My friend on the local TV station couldn't believe it. I managed to get him to agree not to identify me in exchange for broadcasting the story. It meant I had to allow my legal highs to be mentioned openly for the first time, though. Up until then they had been something that was kept strictly under the radar and was known only to younger people in Tel Aviv.

'I was naturally worried because I didn't want to rub the authorities up the wrong way. At that time I believed that by keeping everything low-key no one would bother trying to shut my operation down. Now here I was, having to expose myself to the world in order to get this gangster off my back. It seemed like a no-win situation but I knew I had to go through with it. I had no choice.'

Avi's exposure of the mobster's attempt to muscle in on his business never made it onto the local TV because Avi instead used the footage to get the gangsters to pull away from him. He explained: 'By threatening to expose the gangster I ensured he would never come back to me again because he wouldn't want to take the risk that I might "out" him properly. I heard from a couple of guys that this gangster was furious and wanted to hurt me but, again, he kept away from me for fear of being exposed. I was very, very lucky.'

And there was a very unexpected 'spin-off' from the story, as Avi explained: 'Word about my legal highs spread even faster than before. People emailed me asking for samples, so I set up a proper website instead of just supplying local traders. The orders went up ten times in the space of two months. Being threatened by those gangsters turned out to be the biggest blessing in disguise for me.'

Avi eventually sold out his business after 'being made an offer I could not refuse'. He explained: 'I allowed a couple of genuine businessmen, not criminals, to buy me out on condition they let me continue to produce new legal highs for them. After all, I am a scientist and the place I love to be in is the laboratory. I was paid a fortune, enough money to support my family for the rest of our lives, so producing new legal highs has become almost like a hobby to me. I enjoy the challenge of coming up with something brand new that skirts around the legal system.'

Today, Avi is a renowned member of the legal-high underworld. He explained: 'Sure, I have a reputation inside the industry and sometimes it's tempting to start up a fully-fledged business all over again. But the legal-high marketplace is much bigger today than when I first started out. The competition is fierce. But I'm still making a fortune out of this business and I've managed to stay alive as well!'

Avi refused to discuss specific products and their ingredients because he doesn't want to help the 'opposition' but he says he is very content with his job and has no plans to 'retire' from the legal-high game in the near future. He explained: 'I'm perfectly set up here. No one bothers me. I am incredibly careful to make sure that my team are hand-picked and extremely trustworthy. I don't want to take risks and I certainly don't consider myself to be a criminal. I am a scientist who has managed to create my own products, which have given many people great enjoyment. Why would I want to do anything else?'

CHAPTER 2

DAVID

A self-contained room with no windows is David's work-place for most of the year. He helps turn Avi's potent 'recipes' into narcotic reality. He's part of a three-man team of former students who blend the substances and in some cases even try them out. David works under great pressure from Avi who expects – and demands – a fast turnaround of product.

David talked about his family, who've been scientists for three generations. He told me of his dream that such sub-stances will become available across 'normal' shop counters throughout the world. As David continues his work in the steamy, hot laboratory, the relaxing sound of soft world music flows from the overhead speakers.

'I never thought I'd end up in this type of business,' said David. He was recruited by Avi from a local university through a friend of a friend who knew of Avi's designer drug production line. 'Obviously I knew all about legal highs because many young people here in Israel use them and we like to think we were consuming them long before most of the rest of the world.

'Avi was known to people who took legal highs as this mythical figure who was getting away with producing some really cool stuff. It's no surprise that here in Israel illegal drugs were virtually impossible to get hold of because our borders are sealed tight thanks to the constant threat of terrorism. No wonder legal highs thrived in this country. They were the perfect alternative to traditional illegal drugs like coke and heroin.'

David, however, runs a tight ship. He explained: 'We are very careful who we talk to about our role in the production of legal highs. Everything has to be kept secretive here. Avi would fire us immediately if he thought we were talking to the wrong sort of people. We all know that the authorities would shut us down and send us to prison if they could prove any of our products were illegal. It's a minefield out there and we are stepping round the explosives all the time.'

David's associates in the lab are all scientifically qualified and he said that working for Avi was 'a great way to learn how to carry out chemical research whatever the end product.' He explained: 'I'm on a learning curve here. We experiment with all sorts of substances but we try our hardest to make sure they are all safe for the consumer. Listen, I test a lot of this stuff myself at weekends and I never rubber stamp any proper production of a new legal high until I am happy that it's safe.'

David is about as far removed from the stereotypical image of a drug dealer as you could ever come across. His parents are academics and he himself was brought up in what he describes as a 'happy middle-class home' in one of Tel Aviv's most affluent suburbs. But he admits that he always yearned for some kind of adventure and Avi has certainly provided that for him.

'None of us consider ourselves to be criminals. We are scientists doing what we know best. Is it any different if you are developing new forms of Viagra or anti-depressants? I think not. Listen, I've always been the risk taker in my family. I like to have fun too, and that's how I first got involved with taking legal highs. I'm fascinated by the way they affect different people and I like the fact that they can sometimes be very helpful when it comes to psychological problems. D'you realize that some of the substances that I have helped produce have made a lot of people's lives much happier?'

David refused to say how much Avi paid him but he said it was 'a very generous salary' and that he also gets bonuses for large sales of any specific products he's been involved in developing. 'If a particular product works really well then we get literally tens of thousands of orders from wholesalers all over the world. It shows us that we've connected with our customers and that is very important to me.'

David and Avi refused to allow me to examine their lab closely because, they claimed, the other 'technicians' did not want to be exposed to any publicity. David explained:

'They're a little shy about their involvement in this business. That's completely understandable since they're highly qualified scientists, who're working here to make some extra income. If their involvement became public knowledge it would affect their chances of working for one of the big corporations in later life.'

But the most closely guarded secret of all is the database of customers who use Avi's products. David is understandably cagey about that subject. 'We have big customers from all over the world because there is a powerful word of mouth when it comes to legal highs. Avi is renowned on the Internet for coming up with new creations which mirror illegal drugs and provide almost identical highs.

'That makes his products incredibly popular. But we would never reveal any of the names of those customers except to say they come from all four corners of the globe. In a sense, our products are also providing an income for those factories in places like China and India where they churn the actual ingredients out before selling to people like us. But they don't want to be publicly linked to legal highs, either. This business is a don't-see, don't-tell kind of game.'

David refused to elaborate on the identity of those suppliers of certain key ingredients but he did concede: 'As I've already said, the majority of these suppliers are based in China and India.' Why those two countries in particular? 'I guess it's because it's cheaper to set up factories in those places and of course labour is very cheap too.'

Profit margins at all stages of the development of legal highs are yet another closely guarded secret but David did admit that Avi often sells on his formulas for certain legal highs for 'a huge lump sum plus a percentage of all the subsequent sales'.

He explained: 'A big fee is demanded upfront on the basis that unless a potential wholesaler is prepared to invest his cash in advance then he probably isn't going to be a decent, honourable customer for us. The idea behind a royalty rate based on actual sales is purely an incentive to ensure that what we produce is of good enough quality to become a proper, in-demand legal high.'

David – who has worked for Avi for two years – admitted he has ambitions that lie 'way beyond' Avi's legal-highs lab. 'I think Avi is very realistic about how much longer he can continue to operate,' he told me. 'There will come a time when others will probably overtake us and maybe that will be the time to quit while we're ahead. I don't plan to stay in this business for ever, either. I'd like to put the skills I have learned in this trade to help develop chemicals for commercial companies.'

David is, however, well aware of the attempts by criminals to muscle in on Avi's business. 'It's no big surprise that criminals try to take over our operation,' he pointed out. 'We must have cost them a lot of money in lost revenue from drugs like cocaine and hash and they seem to have difficulty dealing with the concept of drugs that can be produced "on site", so to speak. And of course, ultimately, they see legal highs as just another licence to print money and they want a piece of the action for themselves.'

As a result Avi employs the services of six former Israeli Special Forces soldiers as 'back up' just in case any of Tel Aviv's notorious gangsters decide to pay a visit. David explained: 'It only happens a couple of times a year but it's quite scary and we have to have these ex-soldiers on standby to show that we will not be pushed around. But so far it seems to have been a very effective deterrent.'

David also admitted that he himself had been approached by a 'criminal organization' to leave Avi's operation and set up a new lab financed entirely by a Tel Aviv cartel. 'I got home late one night and found two guys waiting in a car for me outside my family's house. I thought they were going to kidnap me when they jumped out of their car after I arrived in a taxi. But they tried to make light of it all and said they wanted to employ me for a lot of money and tried to persuade me to go with them to meet their boss.

'I was stunned at first but somehow I managed to talk my way out of it by explaining to them that I simply did not know how to make specific products because Avi kept all that sort of stuff a closely guarded secret. At first they refused to believe me and tried to force me to go with them but then I made out I was tempted by their offer but asked for some time to think it over. I was amazed they then let me out of the car without any more threats.'

David ignored several calls on his mobile from the gangsters over the following few days. 'They must have got the message that I didn't want to work for them because they stopped phoning me after a while. I was relieved but Avi said they might come again and he was right.'

David says he believes the same criminals then organized a burglary of Avi's lab. 'I'm pretty certain it must have been them because they did it soon after my encounter with them. During the burglary they took a few reference books and one of the office laptops but there was nothing about the ingredients on either, so they were pretty much wasting their time.'

David admits that Avi then sent three of his bodyguards round to see the gang to 'let them know that we knew they were behind the burglary'. He explained: 'We never heard another word from them or any other gangsters after that. It was a smart move on the part of Avi.'

David said that since then, the biggest problem facing the lab had been the local police. 'The police would dearly love to prosecute us,' he asserted. 'They see Avi as an evil drug baron taking advantage of all his young customers and employing us as the equivalent of his dealers. But nothing could be further from the truth. Avi not only tests the produce himself but he tries to put people off using his legal highs if he feels they won't be able to cope with the effects.'

However, David admitted there had been 'one or two near disasters' while testing new legal highs, despite what he describes as their fail-safe system. 'What happened sort of proves how seriously we take the safety of users,' he explained. 'There have been a couple of close shaves while we were testing out our products. On one occasion, I had a seizure after trying our own version of a new Ecstasy-type powder called MDMI. It was a bit scary because I thought I hadn't taken a big amount.

'About fifteen minutes after consuming it, I started feeling this baking sensation inside my body. It felt like someone had switched on an oven inside my body. My skin was burning from the inside. I was sweating buckets and I was having real trouble speaking. I didn't know what to do but I presumed it would pass eventually so I just drank a lot of water and waited for it to go away but it didn't. The heat inside me was increasing and the burning sensation was really freaking me out.

'Then after another five minutes I began itching all over my body and I was soon scratching at my stomach and arms so hard that I was drawing blood. I didn't even realize I was bleeding at first. It was only when I looked down and noticed blood on the sleeve of my shirt that it dawned on me that something very bad was happening.

'Moments after that my head felt as if it was rolling and I went into a complete spin and collapsed on the floor. I don't remember anything else for about fifteen minutes because I was out cold for that entire time. When I came to, Avi and another technician were standing over me both talking on the phone to try and get the paramedics. But by the time they arrived I was completely recovered and it felt as if nothing bad had even happened.

'Avi and I later re-examined that product and found that

the measurements were way too big when it came to the main ingredient. We decided to abandon that product altogether and develop something more gentle. You see, the guinea pig system works!'

David then talked in detail about another disturbing incident: 'On another occasion one of the other lab technicians volunteered to take a new product we had just developed called Kocaine. He snorted it and reported that it was very painful on his nostrils. Then his nose began to bleed uncontrollably and we had to lie him down to stem the flow of blood. That nosebleed lasted for five hours, which is obviously not normal and we knew that if this happened to our customers word would soon get out and the product would be "blacklisted" on the Internet and when that happens it can have a very serious effect on business.

'So we went back to the drawing board with the Kocaine product and completely re-examined our formula and decided to stick to much more traditional ingredients. But we were so freaked out by what it did to the lab technician that we even renamed it because it was so closely associated to that dangerous incident.'

Israel may have been ahead of the game to start with, but it is not by any means the only hotbed for legal-high inventors and producers.

CHAPTER 3

DANIEL

They call him 'The Professor' in the UK's legal-high under-world but the name he insisted on using for our interview was 'Daniel'. He's one of a bunch of 'underground researchers' who live and breathe drug development both on and off the Internet. Finding him was tougher than tracking down any old-fashioned drug baron and persuading him to talk was even harder. Yet this quiet, unassuming boffin-type in horn-rimmed glasses claimed he had the skills to create any drug that the world might require.

Many inside the UK's shadowy legal-high business had told me Daniel was one of the most influential figures in the 'marketplace'. His most highly prized invention had, accord-ing to my sources, been a legal high called Methoxetamine, which hit the Web in 2010. This product, known to most as MXE, was said to be more potent than its 'parent', ketamine, which is generally used as an equine anaesthetic but has

become prized by drug users for its ability to deliver a supposed out-of-body experience. But like many other creatives,
Daniel needed a commercial 'helping hand' to turn his
potent discovery into a highly valuable product which could
be mass produced in enormous numbers.

A legal-high firm in the UK took Daniel's design, and had
it synthesized by a legitimate Hong Kong laboratory. Within
months, MXE was being distributed all over the world and
had been hailed by clubbers and Internet websites as one of
the most potent legal highs on the market. In the course of
the following year it had been outlawed in the UK, but MXE
continues to earn fortunes for its inventor and those financial backers to this day.

'I'm just a hard-working nerd,' said Daniel in an interview
that had to be carried out entirely through an intermediary.
'I enjoy the process of inventing new legal highs. I'm not
even in it for the money really. I'm just intrigued by the
whole drug scene and it always struck me that there must
be ways to make better drugs than the ones that are out
there. I mean to say, cocaine is nothing like it once was.
You're lucky if it is ten per cent pure these days. Ironically
all the substances used to stretch it out are chemical not
organic like the original product. So where is the line
between that sort of cocaine and legal highs? There's not
much between them.'

In order to meet Daniel, I had to talk to three separate
contacts and even then he would only agree to participate if
my questions were put in an email. I would then have to

await emailed responses to my questions via a third party. 'I hate hiding behind all these people but I have no choice,' Daniel insisted. 'In the eyes of the police, I'm some sort of evil drug baron but all I do is experiment with stuff and see what comes out the other end. I always try to take my own drugs. I would never dream of expecting anyone to take anything that I had invented until after I had tried it first.

'Of course I've made a lot of money out of my inventions but essentially I look on myself as the same as those old hippies back in the sixties who wanted to spread the word about LSD. Many of the drugs I've developed are safer than the other legal highs out there. You see, I understand chemical compounds a lot more than most people and I don't ever tell my financial backers that I'm cooking something new up until after I have invented it.

'I don't want to be pressurized because that's how mistakes are made. I take my time and I only ever use chemicals that I believe are safe for human consumption. This is important for many obvious reasons but you have to realize that thousands of miles away in places like China and India they're knocking out so-called new legal highs without any consideration for human life. They are giving this business a bad name.'

But Daniel then admitted: 'To be honest about it, I also relish the cloak and dagger aspects of inventing new legal highs. It's a secretive world, which adds to all the excitement of life. What's the harm in that? I'm treated with kid gloves by my financiers because they don't want to lose me to any rivals. As a result I enjoy a pretty nice life with just the right balance of risk and excitement and job satisfaction.'

Daniel refused to divulge where his UK laboratory was based, except to say it was 'somewhere in south-east England'. He explained: 'I'm more worried about rivals breaking in and stealing my new inventions than being raided by the police. The legal-high industry has turned into a very competitive business. You have to keep one step ahead of everybody else or your product will end up never selling in big numbers.'

Daniel claims he's been approached by rival legal-high suppliers to work as their 'research chemist' but he declined all their offers. 'I knew if I went and worked for someone else the pressure would be really piled on and it would all end in tears. The guys I work for are calm, professional and leave me alone most of the time. It's just a business to them and I am allowed to do whatever it takes to come up with new products on a regular basis. I rarely even have to meet the financiers and if, God forbid, the police did ever come calling they'd find it hard to connect me to any of the products sold on the Internet.'

Daniel said he'd told his parents and girlfriend he worked as a financier in the City of London because he didn't want to expose them to any danger. 'It might sound dramatic but whether one likes to accept it or not, I'm working in an underground industry. I don't want my family or girlfriend to know what I do because then it keeps them separate from everything. No one will harm them if they know they know nothing.'

He continued: 'Certain aspects of this industry change literally by the day. D'you realize the police could raid my lab one day and announce that the chemicals I had just produced were made illegal that very morning? That could end up with me facing a prison sentence for developing them. If they'd come twelve hours earlier they wouldn't have been able to do a thing.'

It was hard to get any really meaty details from Daniel because of the indirect nature of my interview with him, conducted through emails. But it was clear he is considered a 'very big player' in the legal-high underworld. He even told me I was the first person he'd ever talked to about his 'profession'. He explained: 'Look, another chemist friend of mine who works for a smaller outfit allowed a reporter to interview him once and within a day of his article appearing in a newspaper he had the police knocking on his door. I don't need to publicize what I do. The Internet and word of mouth does that all for me. My main aim is to keep a low profile and keep coming up with legal highs that can be enjoyed around the world. That is a reward in itself.'

As Daniel explained: 'Legal highs are not going to go away any time soon unless countries decide to legalize drugs and use the taxes to cure addiction. Yes, that sounds very twisted but it's just about the only win-win scenario that can possibly come out of all this.'

Meanwhile, Daniel claimed he was on the verge of

developing the 'nearest thing to real cocaine you will ever find.' I pointed out that virtually every legal-high website made similar claims about their synthetic equivalents to cocaine. 'I know, I know. But I am being deadly serious here. There are numerous other legal-high producers out there trying to develop a substance that can provide the taker with all the same highs as cocaine. It would be a gold rush situation once word got out that such a substance genuinely existed. The effect on the worldwide cocaine market would be phenomenal.'

Daniel continued: 'The trouble is that once someone truly cracks the cocaine market then the criminals will come out in full force and there could be a bloodbath because they see cocaine as their domain, their industry and they will not be happy if all those vast profits are destroyed by a bunch of geeky chemists.'

Meanwhile, others inside the business say the biggest danger comes from the Chinese, who are trying to swamp the world with their own, often poisonous versions of those same legal highs. It's a potentially deadly situation.

China's role in the worldwide legal-high phenomenon has driven the unprecedented levels of demand for those drugs in the West. For the past ten years, the Chinese laboratories have largely restricted themselves to exporting the chemicals needed to manufacture legal highs, but recently they've exponentially increased production of their own, often lethal, brands in order to rack up even higher profits.

Dozens of laboratories and factories across China produce narcotics without any real interference from the state. Many firms acquire a government licence with the genuine intention of selling cosmetics or prescription drugs. But after receipt of the licence there is no enforcement or inspection by the authorities to see that the rules are being adhered to – and that's where the legal-high trade comes in.

These firms will tell the Ministry of Environmental Protection (MEP) that they're in the business of producing pharmaceuticals, while in almost the same breath assuring the China Food and Drug Administration that they are doing nothing more suspicious than making research chemicals. 'There is no collaboration between those authorities and no inspection enforcement, so companies in China can manufacture these chemicals without any regulatory challenges,' says one expert.

It's not just officials who are wilfully turning a blind eye. Large numbers of entrepreneurial Chinese businesses are fully aware that a whole range of substances they sell in bulk are used to produce drugs, but they say it is not their problem. As one expert on China explained: 'As far as they're concerned all they do is sell the chemicals, what the customers decide to do with them is none of their business.' Drug dealers are stockpiling these designer chemicals and in some cases are even entering into partnerships with the Chinese gangsters connected to the laboratories and factories churning out the new compounds that allow everyone involved to stay one step ahead of any new updated drug legislation.

The driving force behind it all is, naturally, profit. It was inevitable that much of the manufacture of legal highs would shift to China because production costs were and still are extremely cheap. These days, with Beijing part-liberalizing its economy, China's trade with the West has opened up despite the lack of real infrastructure to deal with corrupt Customs officials and local government. The combination of a dynamic and ever-growing market along with an almost complete lack of regulation is a perfect fit for the legal-high business model. Today, brand new or seldom-seen drugs appear from China with greater frequency than ever before.

Chinese producers constantly boast that their companies are shipping huge amounts of legal highs to the rest of the world. Even the notorious mephedrone – banned across the Western world in 2010 – can still be purchased in China.

More sinisterly, scientists in China have also made serious inroads into the legal-high market by developing their own synthetic drugs – altering the molecules of one psychoactive to produce another with similar properties. By constantly changing the chemical structure of their products, these businesses avoid detection and the long arm of the law. The result is a new breed of readily available legal-high drugs, hard to control and of dubious quality. Law enforcement officials in the US and UK have been scrambling to deal with ways to handle the menace of Chinese legal highs for many years.

Behind the alarm shared by governments across the world is an awareness that, due to the nature of their manufacturing and their dangerously obsolete laws, the Chinese have failed to effectively implement any proper form of product control.

This means that what is sold as, for example, a new legal high called 'Synthetic Mollys' could very well be anything from rat poison to drywall. In addition to this, there is no guarantee of how much of a specific chemical is contained in each dosage, which can lead to overdoses and death.

It seems to the outside world that Chinese chemists continue to design numerous chemicals which mirror the 'good' of a drug high, with no concern for immediate safety or long-term effects. Dozens of labs have sprung up, mainly in north-eastern China, which supply websites specializing in legal highs as well as directly shipping to head shops in the West.

One kilogram of a legal, synthetic marijuana substitute can be purchased for just over £1,000 in China. The purchases are usually shipped via FedEx and UPS to eager users from around the globe. That one kilogram would provide a million doses, which could then be sold legally, for around £25,000. Customs have no power to confiscate it. But if any of these legal highs do end up being seized then most labs and producers in China are happy to resend the drugs for free. 'That shows what an enormous, profitable business this is for China,' said one expert.

One of the recent 'favourites' emerging from the Chinese labs is 25I-NBOMe, a hallucinogenic compound that's part of the -NBOMe series. Like the others in the series, 25I-NBOMe is ineffective if taken orally, and is more commonly diluted before being administered via a nasal spray or inhaler. The other, more dangerous method of ingestion is to drip the liquid on to patterned and perforated blotter paper, passing it off as LSD.

Each gram contains a minimum of 2,000 doses, making it alarmingly easy to overdose. By way of comparison, 1 gram of the original Ecstasy drug MDMA usually provided eight to ten doses. And whereas LSD will not kill, even when taken in excess, these Chinese-produced drugs have the capacity to be lethal.

Thanks to inconsistent extradition laws, Chinese chemists can still legally brew up murderous concoctions that have the potential to kill hundreds if not thousands, and there is nothing that any other government can do about it. In a desperate attempt to control the influx, the Chinese government belatedly claims to be now trying to ban the import of the chemical chains needed to create banned legal highs such as mephedrone. On 1 September, 2013, China proclaimed that mephedrone was a 'category I psychotropic substance', which meant anyone importing or exporting it needed a special manufacturing licence. But at the time of writing (August 2014) it seemed that those businesses were still able to obtain the necessary paperwork with great ease.

Customs officials at London's Heathrow Airport recently seized a large shipment of white powder from China that was labelled 'glucose' but contained mephedrone. As one other expert pointed out: 'That sums up the situation with China. These sorts of substances always find a way through because the Chinese themselves don't bother to check on anything that is leaving their shores. There is even a line of thought that says the Chinese are perfectly happy to provide the Western world with "poisons" as it gives them a clear sense of superiority. Maybe the Chinese are softening us up before they come in for the kill?'

CHAPTER 4

TE

Te is dressed in a designer suit complete with Church's brogues imported from England. He runs a highly professional company in which a team of secretaries march up and down the main open-plan office carrying samples and price lists. Te smiles all the time and seems to burn up so much energy one wonders if he ever samples any of the dozens of legal highs he produces from his factory. But then Te is a classic example of the new, moneymaking spirit of modern China. He claims the only time he ever sits down is when he invites overseas clients to join him at his highly polished teak desk to share a drop of his favourite brand of Scotch whisky.

Te, thirty-eight, likes to 'keep an eye on' his shiny new Lexus, which sits parked right outside the window of his ground floor office in a nondescript Chengdu skyscraper. In a British context Te, who regularly works late into the night, would be considered a workaholic, but if spending time away from his family bothers him, it doesn't seem to show in his relentlessly cheerful disposition. However, the permanent smile seems designed to make you forget that he's in possession of a razor-sharp business brain, which has helped transform this humbly-born former science student into a legal-high king.

Te is immensely proud of how he has built this company up from nothing just four years ago into one that brazenly supplies countless thousands of British youngsters with substances that in some cases are as likely to kill them as they are give them a high. Te sounds icily detached when he discusses his latest range of products that, he boasts, are rapidly taking over from mephedrone as the new market leaders in the business.

Te's laboratory is deliberately conveniently located within easy range of the city's international airport and biggest train station. It's staffed with a feverishly busy gang of fresh-faced young scientists hard at work trying to develop new products.

He says his neighbours include some of the biggest names in the global pharma business and clearly considers his operation to be just as legitimate. Te admits he personally develops new legal highs that are then mass produced at a factory with a little under a hundred workers in an undisclosed location 'a long way from the city'. Te claims that his company manufactures and ships thousands of kilograms of drugs to Britain, the US and many other countries every month.

LEGAL HIGHS

Te is one of the first Chinese producers of legal highs ever to talk openly about this secretive business. Te insists, naturally, that he is nothing more than a hardworking businessman selling highly commercial products in great demand in other parts of the world. He refused to discuss it with me but clearly authorities in China also do not much care about the legalities behind producing legal highs. Chinese officials have adopted an ambiguous position with regard to the trade. They're careful about being seen to lend official support to these enterprises, but on the other hand it's clear that Beijing has deliberately encouraged the setting up of 'chemical research' businesses specifically designed to cash in on the West's obsession with illegal and now legal narcotics. And many allegedly private companies similar to Te's have been given sophisticated equipment to enable them to provide more advanced research and manufacturing capabilities than most Western companies have with the exception of some of the pharmaceutical giants of the US, Canada and Europe – none of whom would ever allow their facilities to be used to develop legal highs.

Some believe the Chinese authorities have sanctioned the production of legal highs because they are undoubtedly damaging to the user-countries, many of whom are China's traditional Western 'enemies'. In other words, China is making billions out of a vast global business that has the chilling potential to damage the health of millions of people.

Te laughed when I mentioned this theory but it's difficult not to be suspicious about China's ultimate goal. He then clinically outlined the production process and tried to answer fears about the lack of testing of such products.

My interview with Te took place after weeks of negotiation mainly over Skype and by email. I approached him as a potential purchaser for a wide range of his legal-high concoctions. Then I used the strength of our new business relationship to try and get him to open up about the legal-high trade and how the Chinese seemed determined to provide the vast majority of the product needed for this so-called business.

Te explained: 'We don't call them legal highs. To us, they're products. What happens to them after they leave China is not our concern.' Te constantly defended his huge output of legal highs and associated substances from his factory hidden away in China's sparsely populated north-west region, which is roughly the same size as Western Europe. He spoke perfect English because, as he admitted, virtually all his customers spoke in that language. There were moments during my interview with Te when his voice resembled a robot as he gave out cold, clinical measured answers to a whole range of tricky questions. 'We in China believe in providing whatever the customer requires. It doesn't matter what it is we are manufacturing as long as there is a demand and you are happy.'

Before moving into the legal-high business, Te had been the manager of a toy factory. He alluded to the fact that he was 'head hunted' because of his management skills and then encouraged to set up a brand new factory for 'scientific research'. He refused to confirm if he was the real owner of the legal-high business or whether he was fronting up for someone else. He explained: 'There are many new and exciting opportunities here in China with new businesses and factories being opened virtually every day. We have embraced Western capitalism with great energy and enthusiasm.'

Initially Te ignored my questioning on the trickier subject of the damage legal highs inflict on people's health but he eventually admitted: 'We know these substances can be dangerous but there is a great demand for these sort of substances in the West. We can produce them cheaply and quickly, so why not? It is up to the people who take them. It's their decision. We play no part in that.'

Not surprisingly, Te and all the other Chinese-based factories that I contacted openly about legal highs refused point blank to allow any actual visits to their sites, probably because many of these so-called 'factories' were nothing more than hastily built corrugated tin shacks located on barren wasteland. Te, however, insisted this was not the case. 'My factory is a brand-new building. It is extremely clean and well stocked with equipment. We recognize that there is a big demand for this type of product and we aim to supply the best quality for the lowest price.'

The worldwide ban on mephedrone and its derivatives as well as a number of other compounds have ensured that Te and other Chinese legal-high producers always have to keep one step ahead of the game. They even have 'contacts' within China's Customs to ensure the drugs enjoy a safe passage to the West. Other levels of corruption enable these businessmen to create and prepare new drugs to deliberately dodge Western classifications and continue to offer profitable legal kicks in the UK, US and Europe.

'We are in the business of making money,' explained Te. 'I sometimes hear about people dying from taking this stuff but that is the risk they choose to take. We do not force them to take these substances. It is their choice.'

With packages from India and particularly China now the subject of routine suspicion from British authorities, Te revealed that his company employed a practice common among Chinese legal-high kingpins. It's a startlingly simple but effective device that might be compared to money laundering. The products are sent via countries in Europe that don't have as stringent Customs controls as the UK. So a package will be initially conveyed to, for instance, Spain, before being resent to Britain. It's a small amount of effort that Te has found saves them and their clients a huge amount of effort in the long run.

'You tell me any other business that would do that?' he asks. 'That is why we have so many customers in countries like the UK. There is little or no risk for them.'

Te assured me that business had trebled over the past two years. 'Demand for this stuff is incredible. I like it! We make lots of money.'

Indeed it is money that motivates Te, who admitted that he lived for the next deal. Like the vast majority of his compatriots, he wasn't tempted to try his products for himself.

'People in China have no interest in legal highs. We wonder why the rest of the world is so obsessed with getting high. The biggest vice here these days is gambling but even that requires you to stay sober.'

Te claimed that recently he'd been approached by 'three or four' British 'entrepreneurs' wanting to go into partnership in order to produce big quantities of specific legal-high products. 'But why would we want to go into partnership with people outside China?' asked Te. 'It makes no sense.'

Back in the UK, a number of similarly business-savvy individuals have spotted the long-term potential of legal highs and started to make relatively big investments in the substances needed to produce the most popular legal highs.

CHAPTER 5

GERALD

Gerald owns 'at least' three laboratories 'somewhere in Europe' where legal highs are designed and then produced. He openly admitted his investment in this business is driven purely by an obsession with profit but he likes to keep the details vague. Gerald considers himself nothing more than a wealthy 'financier' investing in 'an exciting new opportunity'. He refused to discuss the dangers of legal highs and, instead, talked about the sales of his products and how the Internet had enabled him to reach out to a potential marketplace of hundreds of millions of customers.

It is estimated that within the next two years, the worldwide trade in legal highs will net $5 billion a year and provide a livelihood to hundreds of thousands of people.

'I've always had a sharp business brain,' explained Gerald. 'I see opportunities and I take them. The legal-high trade is no different to, say, retirement homes in that sense. They're both ever-expanding markets. On the one hand you have people living longer in old age and on the other you have young people wanting to enjoy themselves without breaking the law.'

Despite his belief that legal highs are a legitimate business, Gerald (like so many featured in this book) insisted that he would only agree to an interview if his real name was not used. 'It's a tough one but I know that there are a few people on the edge of this business with criminal inclinations and the last thing I want is one of them to come knocking on my door. Also, I believe the police do take a close look at people in this business and I don't want to rub them up the wrong way.'

He continued: 'If you'd asked me about legal highs five years ago I wouldn't have had a fucking clue what you were talking about. I'd just sold an estate agent's business for a tidy sum and was on the lookout for something new and challenging but I never thought I'd end up investing in this strange old game.'

Gerald says he 'stumbled' upon legal highs when he met a London nightclub owner at a dinner party hosted by an heiress in London's Notting Hill. 'I got talking to this guy and he said to me that the legal-high trade was about to explode onto the scene. He said it was a dream come true for people like him because it meant that "drugs" could be openly sold inside his nightclubs without breaking any laws.

'I didn't really know what he was on about at first. Then I started to compute what he meant and it all began to make complete sense. This guy hinted that he was planning to open three more nightclubs in the London suburbs where legal highs would be openly offered for sale behind the bar. He also pointed out that the profit margin on most legal highs was about three times that of a pint of lager. Now that got me hooked!

'I asked him a few questions and he started to realize I was pumping him with a view to making an investment, so the cheeky bugger challenged me to invest in those three new nightclubs he was planning to open. I told him straight away that I'd always sworn to avoid businesses such as clubs, restaurants and pubs because they were high-maintenance, low profit-margin businesses on the whole. He laughed at me and then dropped the subject as I'd made it clear I wasn't interested.

'Then just before the dinner party ended, the same guy asked me if I'd feel any different about investing just in the legal-high business. Well, I could see real potential in that because all you needed was the produce and the outlets would come to you. That's what I call a healthy business scenario.'

Gerald says he exchanged phone numbers with the nightclub owner and a few days later accepted an invitation to visit the man's premier nightspot in the West End of London. 'I have to admit I was intrigued and this guy was offering me a night out on the house at a club that I'd seen mentioned in the gossip columns virtually every day, so I went for it.'

Gerald said it proved a real eye-opener: 'I couldn't believe the amount of people in there and the sort of prices being charged – even a soft drink cost £5! But there I was, sitting there with my friend when this stunningly attractive girl dressed in a gold minidress and heels totters up to us with what looked like a tray similar to the type of thing you used to buy ice-creams or cigarettes from when I was a kid. But this tray contained loads of packets of legal highs. Every type, and it was clear from the packaging what illegal drugs they most closely resembled.'

Gerald claimed he'd never taken recreational drugs in his entire life before then but confessed that he dabbled in a legal high that night. 'I'm a careful sort of bloke and I've never felt the need to take drugs but that night I thought to myself I might as well find out what this bloke was on about when he told me all about legal highs at that dinner party.

'I bought a packet of white powder – I forget the name – and my friend ripped it open and we dabbed some of it on our tongues. I was a bit nervous at first but my friend – who'd taken mountains of drugs in the past – assured me it would be okay. Well, within five minutes I couldn't stop rabbiting. It was brilliant fun and you know what? It's never made me want to try any illegal stuff either. But most importantly, my friend reckoned it was better than illegal drugs. Knowing it was legal helped as well because I always try to steer clear of the long arm of the law.'

Gerald says that on the way home that evening he made what he describes as a 'monumental decision'. He explained:

'Having taken that stuff completely legally inside a very high-class nightclub I realized that this was the tip of the iceberg. This stuff was going to push the coke and pot trade down the plughole. No doubts about it.'

The following day, Gerald contacted the nightclub owner and asked him how best to approach this 'new business opportunity'. He explained: 'I needed this guy to give me the "in" so I could ensure I wouldn't be ripped off. I guess in many ways the legal-high trade is no different from an illegal drug business in that sense.

'I promised this guy I'd give him a special deal on every legal high delivered to his clubs if I could get them for a good price wholesale. That was his incentive but what surprised me the most was when I met the character who was introduced to me as "the manufacturer".'

Gerald went on: 'He was a kid in his mid-twenties with horn-rimmed specs and looked more like Joe 90 than a drug dealer to me.' The 'kid' turned out to be a former university science graduate who'd hooked into the legal-high world in much the same way as David and Daniel (featured earlier).

Gerald continued: 'This guy was knocking out legal highs but he had no idea how to properly market them and distribute them. He'd ended up supplying tiny amounts to individual users rather than finding big outlets, which is where I came in. I offered this kid a huge investment of cash [Gerald refused to say exactly how much but he hinted that it was in the region of £200,000] in exchange for him upping his production. I insisted that some of that cash had to go towards a rep who could sell the legal highs to pubs, clubs, even petrol stations around the country.

'Well, I think this kid thought I was potty when I first outlined my business plan but he went away and had a good think about it and came back the next day with a resounding "yes" and we were in business! Soon we were shifting around 5,000 legal-high units a week to various outlets ranging from phone shops to petrol stations. It was fantastic. We'd tapped into a gold rush. I knew my instincts were right and I am just so glad I got in early.'

Gerald has steadily increased the output of his legal-high company thanks to employing two other 'boffins' who are on standby to produce new versions of any legal highs that get banned. The tweaked product is usually ready to go almost before the ink has dried on the fresh piece of legislation. 'Those guys are the key to the business. It's a movable feast in a sense. They produce products from the softer end of the legal-high market so we don't have any problem with banning orders and suchlike. My legal highs are what they say on the packet. Pick-me-ups for people who need a boost. The other seedier end of the legal-high business I have moved away from now.'

However, Gerald accepts that as the popularity of his brand of softer legal highs continues to grow, it is highly likely that he will be overtaken by much larger corporations. 'Look, I know only too well that a lot of big names have been waiting in the wings watching how the legal-high industry develops. Their dream scenario is to start mass-producing these substances in much the same way that cigarettes are produced today. My legal highs are nothing more than tonics really. I sell something called Evodia Rutacarpa which provides great energy. It's easy to handle and works as effectively as a Red Bull. Then there is Buteo superba which is like a very gentle viagra for people who want to pep up their sex lives. I like to think I am in the more legit side of the market, if you know what I mean.

'I've already had one approach from a household name in the food industry but I batted them away because I know that if I can hold out until legal highs become even more socially and commercially acceptable then I'll make enough money to retire a rich and happy man.'

Gerald went on: 'I've built this company up with some clever investing at the right time. I've sat back and watched the explosion in legal highs knowing full well that, sooner rather than later, my company would become a takeover target for one of the big boys. But I've got to be careful not to sell too cheaply so I'm biding my time but I know that a fortune is only just around the corner now.'

Gerald believes that the entire legal-high business is on the verge of 'hitting a pivotal moment'. He elaborated: 'By that I mean that all these banning orders on the heavier substances will run out of steam. Governments can't keep ignoring the popularity of legal highs. They are here to stay and playing these cat and mouse games with the makers of them is turning into a joke. Surely it would be better for everyone to hold their hands up and try to put together a system that allows all types of legal highs to be openly sold as stimulants without all these ridiculous waivers on the packages of the heavier types of legal highs?'

Gerald is convinced that once these issues are solved then the legal-high industry will take over from soft drinks and sweets in sales terms. 'That's why I'm waiting for the biggest payday of all. I know that one of the big food manufacturers will be prepared to pay a fortune for my company when that day comes.'

Meanwhile Gerald says he is enjoying a 'phenomenal return' for his original investment in the legal-high game. He explained: 'I'm what you call a silent investor because I keep my name well away from the actual company and the guys producing these substances know little or nothing about me. But it's high time the whole industry came out from behind the shadows and when that day comes you will see an explosion in the popularity of legal highs.'

He added: 'Look, I'm selling the really soft stuff which has enabled me to get my products into a wide range of shops and onto all sorts of Internet sites. I'm not interested in hallucinogenics and substances like that.'

As if to emphasize the point made by Gerald, I managed to locate some other 'investors' in legal highs who saw the 'business' in much the same way.

CHAPTER 6

GUSTAV

Gustav, forty-nine, is an unusual product of the legal-high system. He openly admits he is supported by a 'fat trust fund' that helped turn him into a self-confessed Ecstasy addict back in the 1990s. But these days, he claims to have invested more than a million pounds of family money into one of the world's biggest legal-high production lines.

At home in his penthouse in Munich, Germany, complete with indoor swimming pool, Gustav recalled the so-called good old days, when he smuggled Ecstasy from Holland into the UK and the rest of Europe. One of Gustav's regular gigs was to fly a shipment over from Amsterdam in a private plane to Essex. Other times, it would be hidden onboard a yacht and sailed down to the Mediterranean party island of Ibiza, the self-appointed home to the rave scene in the 1990s.

But times have changed. These days Gustav has switched to legal highs and invested a large chunk of his family trust fund in a production line that supplies its own version of Ecstasy to tens of thousands of clubbers in many of Europe's capital cities. He openly admitted that those old contacts had come in 'very useful' when he was setting up his new legal-high business.

'I always loved the thrill and energy of working in the Ecstasy trade back in the day,' says Gustav. 'Now I'm using some of those experiences to run a legal-high version and it's a lot less stressful! I don't really need to work because I have a large trust fund thanks to my family's ownership of an automobile parts business based near Frankfurt. But I got into this business in the first place because I was bored and to a certain degree I still am. I need the "hit" of excitement that this provides.

'I first got involved in the Ecstasy business all those years ago because I had a girlfriend who was heavily into E and she knew I had access to a lot of cash. She persuaded me to put some money into an E factory run by a Serbian guy based in Holland. I made ten times my investment back in the space of two weeks, so I was hooked. But I didn't like the risky, law-breaking aspects of the E business because I knew that my family would disinherit me if I ever got arrested by the police. So I only invested occasionally. But when legal highs first appeared in the club scene about ten years ago, I knew they would be the perfect business for me.'

Gustav talks with a fast, machine-gun rattle and his words seem empty, almost cold. He admitted his trust fund had 'flattened' his emotions compared with most so-called 'normal people'. He explained: 'The trouble with inheriting a lot of money is that you lose your appetite for life very quickly. I don't need to earn money so my interest in anything is really based on relieving boredom. I enjoy the thrill of taking a risk and the profits are a bonus as far as I am concerned. The trouble with having a lot of money without working is that it makes you less curious about the world because you don't really need to be friends with a lot of people. It burns the sense of curiosity out of you and that's not healthy, either. Does that make any sense?

'I like to think that by being actively involved in the legal-high business I'm turning myself into being a more experienced, open, curious human being. The guys I do business with say I am very hard because I am not under the same sort of pressure as they are. I am never desperate enough to agree a cheap deal. That can make me hard to deal with sometimes. But it is very effective because I seem to be able to force the prices down with ease. Also, none of them ever try to fuck me over because I am just another spoilt rich kid from the right side of the tracks. They realize that, if I have to, I will simply walk away from a deal.'

Gustav continued: 'I quit the E business long ago when the price of a tab crashed from £20 to about £1. It was a waste of time. Profits were virtually non-existent but the risks were still just as high. It didn't make any sense. But that crash came about because a lot of cowboys were producing vast batches of E with virtually none of the real ingredients needed for them to work. It was madness. The product was useless and simply didn't get people high.

'Around the same time a number of renegade brands of alleged Ecstasy appeared in Europe and the UK and people began dying after taking these tablets. No wonder people fell out of love with E. Legal highs have cashed in on that gap in the drugs market. People feel safer because they're called legal highs but of course they can still be just as dangerous if not taken in moderation.'

Gustav believes there is a clear link between the illegal and legal drug market that indicates that Ecstasy users are often the sort of people prepared to switch to legal highs. 'A lot of these people used to take Ecstasy. They are my prime market and I already knew a lot of them through selling E. So it was a natural, safe step for me to switch to legal highs.'

Gustav also claimed that his background as a 'spoilt rich kid' actually made people more trusting of dealing with him. He explained: 'I'm not desperate to make a deal and people trust me more because of that. I don't come in and rip off buyers. It's simply not my style.'

Gustav also proudly claimed that his legal-high products were just as potent as any version of Ecstasy from the past. 'That's the beauty of legal highs. You can play around with the ingredients until you get just the right mix and then, pow, they work like a dream. I need good word of mouth in this business otherwise people will not take my product.

'In any case, the development of Ecstasy into a legal-high version has been around for a long time but few producers have actually managed to come up with something that hooks people in like Ecstasy did. When I look back on those heady dance-music days it was bloody obvious there was a need for new products that would be perceived to be safer for people to take. What better description could you wish for than "legal highs", eh? People believe they can take drugs without breaking the law. It's the best bit of free marketing you could ever come across.'

Gustav runs his legal-high empire from the comfort of his luxurious £2 million apartment in Munich and admitted he rarely meets any of his actual customers. 'It works like this. I am like a stopping-off shop for a lot of legal-high products. I recommend substances I think work and then club owners, businesses and some very regular users order them off my website. I keep it very low-key and the orders tend to be frequent and moderate because a lot of these club owners worry that by the time they start selling my products in their clubs they may have been already made illegal.

'Mind you, that doesn't always stop them selling my products. They just like to keep everything very discreet so they don't upset the authorities because that could end up getting their clubs closed down. The stupid thing is that if the police or health authorities bothered to actually go inside most of these clubs they'd find my products being sold openly across the bar.'

Like so many of the so-called businessmen involved in the investment side of the legal-high industry, Gustav's big fear is that 'opportunistic criminals' will start muscling in on his company. 'This is a tricky situation. Criminals have been selling illegal drugs for generations but now new substances have appeared which threaten their profits but are legal. I actually keep my business very quiet from most people because if a criminal heard about the profit margins I am achieving, I'm sure he'd come here and try to take over my business.'

Gustav also insisted that a lot of the media coverage about how dangerous legal highs can be are 'scare stories'. He explained: 'It's incredible how many deaths are associated to legal highs when in fact the person who's died has been mixing illegal drugs like cocaine and legal highs together. Now that is plain stupid.

'I admit that the lack of testing of legal highs is a cause for concern but hopefully the longer these products remain on the market the more safe they will become as they get properly tried and tested.'

Meanwhile Gustav predicts problems in the future as Eastern European and Russian gangs begin to wake up to the profits that can be made from legal highs. 'If they start getting involved that will mean violence and bloodshed on the streets of many cities. The only sensible answer is to stop continually banning them. Then they would be able to come out into the open and that would effectively stop these criminals from trying to muscle in.

'Clamping down on legal highs helps the gangsters,' he says, 'because it means they can pretend certain legal highs are illegal drugs to trick people. After all, they are much cheaper than real cannabis and cocaine, so it's giving these criminals even bigger profit margins.'

Gustav, who favours crisp white well-ironed shirts and

drives a top of the range Audi, insists he'd 'never do business' with such criminals. 'I've gone out of my way not to get involved with these characters because I know that once they have you in their circle, they will squeeze you dry and then steal your business. I've heard of some gangsters making massive investments in legal-high companies and these characters have only one aim; to take over those businesses once they've talked their way in.'

And Gustav has this warning for anyone trying to start up a legal-high business. 'There are a lot of amateurs around who try to sound big and impressive on the Web but most of those are one-man bands, who're very vulnerable to a takeover from the real drugs underworld. I even know of some who have fallen for these criminals and their cash and then find they have been turned into virtual slaves.

'There is one guy who ran a legal-high company who disappeared a few weeks after accepting an investment from a gang. I heard they threw him off a bridge and his family were told it was suicide. I'm not going to end up in a box because of this business. It's been good to me but I would step away from it the moment I thought there was a risk to my life or that of my family and friends.'

It seems that a healthy sense of caution is essential if you're in the legal-high business – especially if you're operating out of a country that insists on the death penalty for anyone caught trafficking drugs.

CHAPTER 7

TED

A London-born former timeshare salesman now runs one of Thailand's biggest legal-high production lines. Ted, thirty-four, claimed to have recently cornered a vast new market in south-east Asia and is proud that he has the perfect pedigree to continue to expand his business for many years to come.

Ted first arrived in Thailand in 2008 as part of a mass exodus from Spain's so-called Costa del Crime following the onset of the financial crisis in Spain. At the time, Spanish authorities were also cracking down on the area's gangster residents, who included a large number of British villains. Ted insisted he was not a criminal, although he openly admitted that the notorious timeshare industry could be 'extremely dodgy'. He explained: 'I just reckoned it was time to split from Spain. I'd made a fortune out of the timeshare business and even managed to finance a couple of low-budget movies with some of the proceeds. But I sensed there was growing resentment against characters like me in Spain, who were considered vermin ripping off anyone who came their way. In any case, no one had any money to buy time-share apartments any more, so it was definitely time to go.

'It was also getting very expensive to live in Spain and they'd just hit a crippling recession, which meant property prices were crashing while the cost of living was shooting up. I knew all about Thailand from a couple of my mates who'd gone there straight from Spain. One of them had even set up a new timeshare operation in Thailand which was run on similar lines to the one I worked on back in Spain. All in all, it looked like a land of opportunity to me.

'But I knew timeshare itself had peaked so I decided to look around for some new business opportunities when I got to Thailand. In any case, I wanted to do something more challenging. I bought myself a beautiful house for next to nothing. Then I purchased a couple of warehouses for less money than you'd spend on a lock-up garage in London.

'I'd heard all about the legal-high business through some mates back in the UK and I knew it was simmering. It was a good moment to invest in it.'

Ted then ploughed £100,000 into start-up costs for his own legal-high business. 'If I was going to do it, I wanted to do it properly and be the biggest and best legal-high business in Thailand. It's certainly a perfect place to do it because if you spend money out here and employ locals then everyone is more than happy, whatever that business happens to be. More importantly, I'd already worked out there were loads of potential legal-high customers out there. I only needed a small fraction of that market and I'd be laughing all the way to the bank.'

Ted recruited staff for his warehouses through a local labour exchange. 'Out here they don't even know what the phrase legal highs means. To be frank about it, the six guys I employ here are just grateful to have a job. Not many people in these parts are employed.'

Meanwhile Ted searched the Web for two 'boffin scientist types' to work for him developing new legal highs. 'This was the tricky bit because I knew only too well that if they were useless then they'd either end up killing my customers or ripping them off and I couldn't afford to do either because I wanted plenty of repeat business.'

Then Ted had a stroke of luck. He explained: 'I was skimming through the various legal-high websites and I noticed that one of the biggest suppliers had suddenly shut down and there was a notice offering the site for sale for peanuts. I got in touch with the people behind it immediately and offered to buy the website off them if they could recommend two or three scientists I could use to develop new legal highs. They only wanted a couple of grand for the site, so I was immediately quids in.

'The two guys who were recommended turned out to be very professional characters and the big advantage for me was that they'd already been experimenting for years on various new products and had half a dozen brand-new substances ready and waiting for someone to press the button.

These two guys were students from Pittsburgh and they jumped at the chance of an adventure in the Far East. I got them over here, set them up in an apartment and put them to work. The great thing about them is that they really do enjoy their job. They are genuine legal-high enthusiasts.

'They've been working for me for quite a long time now and I believe they are two of the finest legal-highs technicians in the world. They really know their stuff and they have this wonderful scientific brain when it comes to the logic of each new product. I have treated them well and I believe that one day they'll probably move onto a more legitimate line of business but for the moment they seem very happy.

'After all, they're surrounded by happy, available women, cheap booze, plentiful sun and a beautiful landscape beyond their wildest dreams. Sometimes I take them out for dinner to see how they're getting along and they still act like a couple of teenage schoolchildren but that enthusiasm is a delight to see. If they'd been a couple of boring old has-beens then it would have been reflected in the products they came up with. These guys are innovative.

'They're also hyperactive beyond belief! They come up with new ideas virtually every day. Some of those ideas are completely crazy but others are really clever and the biggest test of all comes when I test out the response to new products on my website. If there is a lot of interest then we immediately press the button and bang out lots of the new product. But the most important thing is that they're young and completely in touch with their customers. I couldn't make this business work without characters like them.'

Ted refused to name his two 'scientists' for fear that they might be poached by rival legal-high merchants. He explained: 'I know that some of my competitors are well aware I have two geniuses on board and they'd love to try and lure them away from me. Also, they want to keep low-key because their families don't even realize what they're up to.'

Ted seems to have it all wrapped up. But he reckons it is never a good idea to kick back in the legal-high business. 'This is an ever-changing market and if I was stupid enough to sit back and watch all the money come rolling in then I'd probably fail to notice when the demands of my customers changed. I have to keep abreast of all the latest developments, otherwise they'll go to another website. It's a tough, highly competitive business and you have to keep one step ahead at all times.'

However, Ted revealed that one vitally important golden rule has helped his business to thrive in Thailand. He explained: 'I don't sell any produce in Thailand. Full stop. Right at the beginning I got talking to a local police chief here and he advised me to avoid selling anything here because they would be considered real drugs and the Thais are obsessively anti-drugs. I mean, they still have the death penalty for drug smuggling here.

'They believe that any mention of drugs in Thailand will be bad for tourism and they rely so heavily on that industry they would close me down and sling me in prison immediately if they believed I was dealing any type of drugs here. It's a small sacrifice and, to be honest about it, I don't blame the Thais one bit. They want their country to be drug free.'

Ted's ultimate aim is to expand his business and open up more legal-high factories in other 'friendly' countries where he can run his operation even more openly. 'But for the moment it's fine here in Thailand. The taxes are low. The cost of living is low and it's given me time to get the business up and running without having to spend a fortune.'

So what about the legal highs themselves? Has he ever taken them? 'No way. I learned the hard way when I was a kid and got a bit, shall we say, caught up in a bit of heroin. I am an addictive personality, so it's better I steer clear of that sort of stuff and pour all my energies into this business. Making money is my drug of choice.'

While dodgy businessmen like Ted happily rake in profits from their carefully run legal-high businesses in places like Thailand, spare a thought for the rest of the world. In Eastern Europe, the legal-high industry is considered a part of the illegal drugs business and often cocaine and cannabis are 'refined' in factories alongside their legal-high 'cousins'.

CHAPTER 8

GIORGI

Giorgi, forty-three, has worked as a criminal all over Europe. But two years ago he returned home to Romania to set up what he believes to be the country's first legal-high factory. It is here that he produces many potentially dangerous substances, most of which are sold openly on the Internet in dozens of countries across the globe.

Giorgi admitted he pays only 'peanuts' to a couple of unemployed Romanian science graduates to concoct substances based on other products he sees on the Internet. He clearly has no idea if they work on users, although he insists they never contain anything that is dangerous to people's health. But the mere fact he met his two 'employees' in a Bucharest bar pretty well sums up the haphazard nature of his operation.

Giorgi's story is both disturbing and predictable. He claimed to be an 'honourable man' mass-producing legal highs and insisted he was responsible about the ingredients. But, ultimately, he is nothing more than a criminal out to make what he thinks will be big bucks.

Giorgi is a classic example of an old-school gangster who's drifted into the legal-high industry and sees little or no difference between it and the illegal drug trade. 'Look, my business is making money. I don't care how I do it as long as I do. I see these so-called legal highs as just another product to sell on the black market. In my eyes, they are no better or worse than drugs like cocaine and cannabis but I try to make sure my drugs are not dangerous because I want my customers in places like England to come back over and over again to buy my products.'

Giorgi first got involved in legal-high production after he visited a relative in the UK. At the time he was running vanloads of heroin that came through Romania from Afghanistan and Turkey. 'I was delivering heroin to these Turkish mafia guys in north London and they treated me real bad and even tried to rip me off by claiming that the vanloads of heroin were short. It was a lie and typical of the way they always tried to trick me.'

Giorgi explained that eventually the Turks accused him of stealing more than half a million pounds' worth of heroin and threatened to put a price on his head unless he paid them back the full value of the drugs. 'That was the last straw. I knew I had to stop working for them or else I would end up dead.

'So I decided I needed to find another business. I knew the

key to it was to be the supplier rather than the transporter. Then I would not face these sorts of threats all the time. One of my cousins in London told me about legal highs. I couldn't believe what he was telling me at first. It seemed too good to be true. They'd only started to come onto the market [it was in 2007] but he told me that they were easy to make and legal! It didn't take much more persuading than that!'

But Giorgi admitted that at first he had 'no idea' what was actually in legal highs and even less idea how to manufacture them. 'I didn't even use the Internet much back then. In Romania, guys like me made our money from importing drugs, women, that sort of thing and the Internet was not part of our business. In any case, I did not trust the Internet. I had heard stories about how the police monitored it and could get enough evidence to arrest people just by recording what they'd written on the Internet. But my cousin convinced me that I needed to recognize that the Internet was like one big street corner for the whole world. If I could find a way to use it to sell my produce then I would make much money.'

Initially, Giorgi ordered a selection of legal highs through the Internet to sample. Then he came up with what he calls his 'brainwave'. He explained: 'I researched the ingredients of these legal highs and realized that most of the substances needed to make them could be bought very cheaply in Romania. That meant I could produce them for very little cost and sell them in big numbers on the Internet without even breaking the law.

'You see, in Romania, no one even today really understands what legal highs are. Sure, things like glue are used by the sewer kids in Bucharest but these new chemical legal highs mean nothing out here and the politicians have no idea that openly available ingredients can be used to make them here.'

Giorgi said that the other important factor was the sky-high unemployment rate in Romania. Giorgi explained: 'I realized I could even get a grant from the government to set up a factory producing legal highs because I would need to employ some people.'

But Giorgi still required one last piece to complete his legal-high jigsaw. He explained: 'I needed specialists. So I started going round all the Bucharest student bars until I found the right people. It was not hard because even students struggle to get work out here.' Giorgi then put his two young recruits to work with strict instructions to closely replicate the most popular legal highs on the market.

'Within one year I was mass-producing all the household names at a fraction of the price they cost from the big Internet companies. In the local community, I'm considered a legitimate businessman providing employment for my import/export firm. My workers never ask any awkward questions either. They're just happy to earn a wage.'

Giorgi went on: 'I love this business. For the first time in my life I'm running something that gives me big respect in the community because I employ people. I'm a local businessman, not a criminal and it's a nice feeling. I can live openly without worrying that someone is after me or that I have ripped someone off and they want revenge. It's probably the nearest thing to being an honest citizen for someone like me. I love it!'

However, Giorgi admitted he's 'had problems' with other criminals trying to muscle in on his business. 'Hey, at first it was all fine. I think the old-fashioned criminals thought I'd gone soft in the head! But then they heard stories about the profits I was making and that seemed to annoy them.

'Soon I received "visits" from one or two of them enquiring about whether I needed their help and offering protection for the factory. Stuff like that. I knew they were after a piece of my profits but I also knew that if I let them have anything they would come back for more and more and more until I was broke. So I stood up to them. I armed myself and employed five bodyguards, also all armed, to travel with me because I knew my life might be threatened.'

Giorgi insisted that the other gangsters got the message 'and left me alone'. He explained: 'Then one day, I got a call from a contact to say that a particularly heavy Bucharest gangster had been shouting his mouth off that he was going to kill me and then take over the business. I knew he was being serious, so I took my own pre-emptive action.'

Giorgi said he then deliberately lured his criminal rival into a trap by making sure all his movements were 'publicized' to the underworld. 'I was fed up of this guy. He had no right to do this to me. I knew I needed to tackle it head on so I waved a carrot at him. Everywhere I went I made sure everyone knew. A few days later, I was travelling in my SUV on an isolated road about fifty miles outside Bucharest when we were forced off the road by two trucks. Three guys jumped out of each vehicle but they didn't realize I had two back-up cars behind me. So as these bad men pulled out their guns my team took up positions by the side of the road and fired back and killed at least two of them. That was the last time they ever tried anything like that.'

The incident garnered so much local publicity that Giorgi claimed he was 'treated with much more respect' after it happened. 'Those gangsters did me a favour because all the other criminals realized I was not a guy to fuck with and I was pretty much left in peace after that.'

Today, Giorgi claims to be producing 40,000 units of various legal-high substances every month and he sells those on to consumers, wholesalers and retailers throughout Europe, South Africa and the US. He explained: 'I have regular customers who seem very pleased with what I supply. These people ask few questions and I hardly ever get any complaints. I need to keep my customers happy because the key to my success is the hardcore of customers who repeatedly order produce from me at least once a month. The UK is the richest market by far. The prices per unit are high and there are more shops and Internet sites selling my produce in the UK than in any other country in the world.'

Unlike businessman Gerald, manufacturer Giorgi does not expect to be bought out by any big corporations in the near future. 'I know this business is short term. I reckon that Romania will probably be forced to shut down factories like mine when they begin to realize what it is that I produce. I'm just taking advantage of this moment in time. Who knows? By next week, another type of industry might take over from the legal-highs trade and I need to keep an eye out on all those sorts of developments.'

Giorgi claimed he deliberately did not travel to the UK these days. 'The beauty of my business is that I don't even need to be in other countries. I can run everything from here in Romania. I know that the police would be interested in me in London because of my past connections to the drug-smuggling trade. I also hear from my friends in the UK that your bank accounts can be raided by the police and the tax people if you're making money from legal highs. I don't understand how that can be since it is not breaking the law but there are some strange rules in the UK which I do not really understand but I don't want to put them to the test so it is better if I just keep away from there.'

Giorgi's plans for the future are unclear. He says he is happy to keep producing the legal highs but he is well aware that he may have to switch to another business at very short notice if the laws are changed. 'I think Romania will end up banning these substances because they will be told to do so by the Europeans. It's only a matter of time but I have enough friends in high places to know I will be given plenty of notice.'

Surprisingly, Giorgi reckons the biggest single threat to his position in the legal-high underworld are the amateur chemists capable of producing their own newly designed narcotics and completely cutting out the middle-men. In both the UK and US they are making a big dent in the market for designer drugs.

CHAPTER 9

VINCE

Vince fancies himself as a bit of a boy wonder chemist, even though he left school at sixteen and has worked ever since as an estate agent in Central London. 'I know it sounds daft but I'd rather make my own legal highs than trust all that stuff out there on the Internet and in the head shops. Chemistry was the only thing I was interested in at school so my attitude has always been: why not have a crack at it myself?'

Vince claims he first got into taking legal highs when he found that the cocaine he was purchasing was 'substandard'. 'Coke is big business in London,' he said. 'Many of the people I work with take it and until recently I was a big consumer. I found it helped make me sharper and improved my ability to pull off big property deals and many of my friends were the same.

'But there came a time when we all started to notice that the quality of the cocaine we were buying was, quite frankly, shit. It got so bad that I started to wonder if the suppliers were cutting it so much that there was no actual cocaine in the stuff we were buying.'

Vince said it was then he 'took the law into my own hands'. He explained: 'I kept back some of a batch of cocaine I'd bought with a friend and we got it analysed and, surprise, surprise, there wasn't a grain of real cocaine in what we'd bought. I was outraged and wanted to take it back to the dealer but my friend calmed me down and pointed out that they would never admit it, so we had a choice: either continue buying the "rubbish" or switch to something completely different. That's when another friend mentioned legal highs. He reckoned there were a couple of products on the market which actually worked better than cocaine itself.

'We tried a few things that passed themselves off as cocaine-type legal highs but they were utter crap. So I phoned a scientist-type mate of mine who I went to university with and asked him if it would be possible to modify the chemical make-up of substances to produce new versions of coke or MDMA that would be totally legal. Yes, he said. It would be easy. Well, it was all plain sailing after that.

'The first batch was just a small amount because I wanted to be sure it actually did what it said on the packet, so to speak. Well, I can tell you it worked a treat. I was so impressed I asked around my friends to see if they all agreed and whether they'd put some money into mass-producing the stuff we'd come up with.

'The key factor was to find a proper location to make a

decent amount of it. That's when I had my first lucky break. I made out I was representing a UK pharmaceutical company and even put a request online for anyone who knew about this particular substance. Loads of people contacted me but they were all fraudulent, which sums up the state of the worldwide web!

'Then I started researching countries outside the EEC with their own chemical industries. Trouble was when I contacted them, very few could speak any English so it was back to the drawing board.'

That's when Vince switched his attention towards India. He continued: 'Three separate companies came back to me and insisted they could synthesize the drug but I had my doubts, especially when they all quoted huge charges. One bloke wanted £35,000, which was outrageous.'

But after endless hours searching the web, Vince was contacted by a friend who pointed him in the direction of a site in China that, superficially at least, had nothing to do with legal highs. He explained: 'They claimed to be selling organic chemicals around the world and that also included offering pharmaceuticals to perfectly law-abiding importers. But I heard how dodgy these sorts of Chinese operations were and that there was virtually no control over them. I knew they had a reputation for adding all sorts to the products, but I thought that this outfit was at least worth trying out given the hassle I'd experienced up until now.

'The Chinese lab I contacted came back within minutes. They tried to make out they were curious about my intentions but it was clear they didn't really care one bit. When money came into the conversation their only interest was whether I would be employing them on a long-term production line. I told them it was for veterinary care and they didn't argue.

'We hammered out a deal there and then and surprisingly there was even a brief conversation about quality control. They even agreed to send me over data confirming the creation of the specific drug I wanted. It only cost a few hundred pounds and it put my mind at ease enormously.

'Well, I was stunned when they took just ten days to get it ready, although it was still in liquid form. Mind you, I could hardly complain since its purity stood at more than ninety per cent. They told me they could use hydrochloric acid to make it look, taste and smell even more like cocaine. Then they shipped it over to the UK.

'Strictly speaking I wasn't breaking any laws. As a result I didn't even have to smuggle it or hide it in any way. Ironically, it was the laboratory in China who insisted on sending it in plain packaging and five days later a plain brown parcel turned up.'

But that wasn't the end of the process by any means, as Vince then explained.

'My next move was to offer the "cocaine" privately to some of my closest friends and associates, all of whom had been very into coke. They loved it and all of them reckoned it worked much better than the crap stuff we'd been buying before I decided to produce a legal-high version.

'That's when I decided to turn it into a proper business. I knew I'd stumbled on something very lucrative, so I decided to get some online reviews for the drug. My intention was to hype it right and create a demand. Well, it worked as smooth as silk. Soon I was knocking it out for £35 a gram. It had cost me less than £2.50 a gram. Not a bad profit margin if I say so myself!

'A few weeks later I was contacted by a couple of really geeky types who said they'd been blown away by my product and asked me if I had any objection to them testing the stuff in their own lab. The results were incredible. These two dudes said it was "high purity" with the onus on high. They praised me for inventing it and even praised the lab in China for doing such a good job. Well, with that recommendation, I decided I should turn this into a serious business.

'Today, I'm still working as an estate agent but I'm making almost as much money out of that one product. But I've decided not to expand in any way. I believe that just so long as I keep it small then nobody else is going to take an interest in what I'm up to. I've managed to produce a legal analogue of an illegal drug. And it really was as easy as I've just described. Maybe it's too easy in some ways and people who do this try to expand out of pure financial greed and then they come unstuck.

'Not me. I am enjoying taking the stuff and selling it. By the time your book comes out there will probably be another cocaine-equivalent legal high out there that knocks spots off my version and I will have gone back to just being an estate agent and no one will be the wiser and, you know what? That's probably the best thing that could happen to me because I don't want to be associated with criminal or dodgy practices. I like my life the way it is and long may it continue.'

PART TWO

HANDLERS/RETAILERS/
DEALERS – UK, USA, SOUTH
AFRICA, JAPAN

*It's not difficult to find things that are controlled, then
devise a minor chemical modification to bring them outside
control. Then you can contact a Chinese laboratory and
they'll happily custom-synthesize it for you.*

Dr John Ramsey, toxicologist
at St George's Medical School, London

The Internet has played an enormous role in helping promote and guarantee sales of legal highs, as well as providing an anonymous testing base for those thinking about taking such substances. As one seasoned legal-high consumer said: 'Back in the sixties and seventies, young people relied on the recommendation of their friends when it came to drugs. These days you can Google the testers and get a whole wide range of opinions on every single type of legal or illegal drug.'

The legal-high explosion would be almost inconceivable without the Internet. Virtually from day one there was a culture of psychonauts sharing the latest recipes of legal highs as well as advice and information based on their experiences of using them. But increasingly, this knowledge is being hijacked by the criminal underworld who regularly monitor the Internet to ensure they're up to speed with all the latest developments, which they can then send to laboratories in places such as China, where – as already revealed in this book – they can then be produced on an industrial scale.

A more recent phenomenon has been the Silk Road, the 'deep' underground site where, providing you have the appropriate Bitcoin finances, you can purchase any substance with relative ease. There are other sites too. One called Bluelight allows access to the most up-to-date information about almost any narcotic substance imaginable from people with direct subjective experience.

So, while the net has undoubtedly helped the legal-high industry expand at an incredible rate, its very openness has created a space for opportunists to try and get a stranglehold on the entire business. Many people who handle, retail and, ultimately, deal in legal highs have emerged out of nowhere in recent years to dominate the worldwide market.

CHAPTER 10

ADAM

The legal-high underworld contains many individuals whose background is steeped in mystery. As one commentator pointed out: 'You haven't got a clue who you're *really* dealing with on the net. Yet people are putting their own lives on the line with substances produced by so-called legal-high experts who deliberately create a false trail. In other words they may not even really exist.'

Take Adam. He's a classic example. This ex-public schoolboy got a degree at Cambridge University and had a career as a high-powered accountant until he was convicted of defrauding a client and received a suspended prison sentence. 'That was the pivotal moment in my life,' explained Adam. 'I was being fast-tracked for a very well-paid job on the board of this City company and then, wham! I got hit between the eyes and found myself out of a job and with a criminal record. I was so scared I didn't even tell my wife and children what had happened.

'For the following year, I pretended to go to work every morning to ensure they didn't find out what had happened. I even managed to persuade my sick and elderly mother to lend me some money so I could continue paying my children's private school fees and appear to have some kind of "income". It was a horrible, stressful time in my life but I felt I had no choice in the matter. The worst thing of all, though, was not feeling able to tell anyone what was happening. I used to go to bed every night and turn over and pretend to go straight to sleep in order to avoid talking to my wife.'

However, Adam admitted, he knew a time would eventually come when he'd have to come clean or find a new way to earn a genuine income. He explained: 'I kept putting off that moment. I'd squeeze some more money out of my elderly mother and then tell my wife my new business was slowly going into profit so she understood that I might not earn much money for a while but eventually I'd make bucketloads of cash. I remember some nights we'd all sit round having dinner together and I'd tell my wife and children how my business was on the verge of making millions. It always made me feel better to say that because there was this look of relief on all their faces.

'You see, I come from a pretty conservative background in the heart of Middle England. The man is expected to work and bring home the bread, so to speak. My father was the same before me. I knew next to nothing about drugs. They were something I had no interest in as a child because I was a hard-working student determined to have a career and a family and nothing much else. I was pretty straight.

'I vaguely remember a few of my friends at school and university smoking pot but that was about it. In fact, to be honest about it, I was pretty snotty towards the druggy set at my public school and then at Cambridge. I couldn't understand why anyone would want to risk their life for something that I had no interest in. I also hated the fact that drugs seemed to make you give up control and control is something I've always liked to have.'

With no job and the 'loans' from his mother rapidly about to dry up, Adam began surfing the Internet trying to find a way to earn some money. 'I was desperate. I knew my mother's bank account was almost empty. I had nowhere else to turn. I needed something easy to get into that would bring a fast return. It seemed to me that legal highs were a lot easier to get into selling than most businesses. The start-up costs were modest. You just needed to find a good, reliable supplier and off you went. At first I didn't really appreciate that the product needed to actually work if I was going to establish any repeat business, which is the key to these sorts of businesses.

'Then I noticed that certain former Eastern Bloc countries were offering very generous subsidies to businesses to set up in their countries as a way to reduce unemployment. So I headed over to Moldova and quickly found an incredibly cheap warehouse to rent. Then I went in to claim my subsidies by presenting a business plan, which included employing eight local people to run the warehouse. They were delighted to have me on board. They didn't really seem to care what sort of business I was going to run from that warehouse.

'I knew I only really needed two or three workers but I wanted to massage the numbers and I knew I'd get much bigger grants if I employed more people. But most important of all, the Moldovans had no interest in legal highs and it was made clear to me that no one would ever attempt to confiscate my products whatever the laws in the rest of Europe and beyond, where all my potential customers would be based.

'I ended up with a grant in Moldova that covered 75 per cent of my start-up costs, including 75 per cent of the salaries I would have to pay my employees for the first year. It seemed like the steal of the century to me.

'I just had to make sure I got my legal-high business idea off the ground rapidly. I soon located what I thought was the best place in China to produce the legal highs I wanted to sell. The warehouse in Moldova became the stopping off point for all my products. In other words my legal highs would never have to go onto UK soil from the moment they were ordered online until they turned up via a delivery service on someone's front door. That meant I was untouchable in the eyes of the laws of Europe.'

Adam, now in his late thirties, started up his business in late 2012. 'It took just three months to go into profit which is amazing when you consider most businesses struggle along for years before they make any money. I fly over once a month to make sure no one is stealing from me and that the workforce are happy but it has all gone incredibly smoothly.'

Adam is today mightily proud of his business and the way it rescued him from unemployment and disaster. 'I consider myself to be just another entrepreneur who has worked hard and used all my skills and experience as an accountant to get this business going.'

However, Adam admitted that he told very few people the real nature of his work. He explained: 'It's no one's business but mine what I do. That's why I don't want my real name used for this interview. I tell all my friends and family that I am exporting computer parts from Moldova and they are all suitably impressed. It's better not to tell people about the legal-high aspects, especially since my family would be rather snotty about that sort of thing. I also have young children and I really hope they never take any drugs.'

Adam refers to his legal-high website as if it is a genuine law-abiding business that puts him up there with the corporate giants of the US and UK. He's even managed to manipulate Google so that his business can be found on the first relevant page of any Internet search for legal highs. 'I know this business may not last for ever but it's certainly saved me from the scrapheap because it's given me back my confidence. I now know how to set up a low-cost business and rake in profits very quickly. I might even branch out into business consultancy eventually because I have picked up so many useful skills along the way.'

Recently, Adam expanded his enterprise and took on a new partner. He explained: 'This guy's background is online retail. He previously ran a business selling refurbished goods on eBay and Amazon. He's a sharp character and he knows the Internet inside out. He reckons we can at least double our profits over the next eighteen months if we use certain clever business techniques.'

Adam refused to reveal what those 'techniques' might be but he clearly considers himself to be as legitimate as any normal business entrepreneur. 'I'm pleased with the way things have gone. Sure, I don't like to advertise the legal-high aspects of my business but it's still a very healthy business and I created all this, so I must be doing something right.'

Adam claimed his legal-highs website earned him more money per year than he was making as a top accountant but he's understandably reluctant to share specific sales figures. 'I don't want to talk about that side of things. I've got a very healthy tax situation and I don't want to rub the taxman's nose in it. Then there is my family to consider. My wife and children would no doubt consider legal highs no better than illegal drugs but, hey, I'm earning a good living and not once has any of them asked me any awkward questions. Sometimes I think my wife must be a bit suspicious but she stopped asking awkward questions long ago and seems to have decided to enjoy the money.'

It's no surprise, given his experience, that Adam's website is as slick and as professional as any other retail website. It takes eight different payment cards, there's an 0800 number for customer service, there's even an online 'help centre' and a live chat function for customers. The business has achieved an ISO9001 accreditation (for quality management systems) and guarantees delivery within one to two working days.

But as Adam explained: 'It's not unusual to see this level of professionalism among the research chemical and legal-high websites that rank highest in Google results. Many are multi-lingual, image-heavy and information-rich, as easy to browse as any big business from IKEA to Tesco's.'

But then Adam and many of the other legal-high online retailers consider themselves legal businesses. 'As long as I always remind the customers that everything they buy is "not for human consumption" and label the products as "research chemicals", "plant food" or "bath salts" to avoid infringing the 1971 Misuse of Drugs Act or the 1968 Medicines Act, then I have done nothing wrong.'

Adam's recent expansion plans also included recently acquiring a rival website, although he admitted that the proliferation of new legal-high websites means competition is increasing almost every day. 'I like to think I've earned my company a good reputation in the marketplace,' he said. 'Repeat custom is important, and loyal customers get discounts and special offers. It's all about providing a good service.'

Then Adam proudly added: 'I offer the best service and the best quality products. Look, a lot of the websites don't even have telephone numbers or email addresses, and even when they do, they often don't answer emails, which is just a basic thing but you'd be amazed how many so-called retailers fail to provide this level of service.'

Quality of product is critical. Adam sends samples of the drugs he stocks in Moldova to labs, then publishes the purity reports on his website. But he refused to reveal who his suppliers were. He explained: 'I don't want someone else trying to undercut me. I always say to anyone who wants to get into this business, "Find your own suppliers and start a relationship with them." It's essential.'

Adam boasts that his big profit margins are achieved because he imports his drugs from China. 'There's a lot of bollocks talked about in relation to China. I went out there and we agreed a deal and I trust them. In any case, they know I'm always testing the produce and if they tried to scam me in any way, I'd simply go and find another supplier.'

Adam also claimed his operation was one of the most logistically sophisticated out there. He ships internationally, though never to the US (too fraught with legal risks). While UK-based warehouses have drug shipments that are often stopped at Customs, he never has that problem in Moldova. 'The Moldovans are desperate to keep foreign businessmen like me happy and they'd never dare stop any of my products as they come in and then go out from the warehouse.

I get little or no interference from the authorities just as long as I keep employing locals at the warehouse.'

Adam likes to believe he is the 'respectable face' of the legal-high business. But there are many others in the trade who look and act more like stereotypical cocaine barons.

CHAPTER 11

MICKEY

Mickey is not your average legal-high merchant by any means. Aged forty-five, he's slickly dressed and has a penchant for loud Gucci shirts and expensive sunglasses. He drives an Aston Martin convertible and boasts that his two children attend one of Britain's most exclusive public schools.

But then Mickey – or Michael as he prefers to be called these days – has history when it comes to legal highs. 'I like to think I am a trendsetter,' he explained. 'I spot the trends and then set them. I've always had a knack for looking into the future and making bucketloads of cash but I reckon that legal highs will provide me with the biggest money pit I've ever jumped into.'

Mickey continued: 'I've dabbled in and out of the illicit drugs trade most of my working life. I've bought shipments of stuff like cocaine, transported them for other people and in my teens I was even a pub grub [drugs] dealer. You could say it's in my blood.'

But all that involvement with illegal drugs pales into insignificance when it comes to what Mickey calls 'the deal of the bloody century'. He explained: 'Like most villains, I looked the other way when legal highs first appeared on the scene about ten years ago. Sure, Ecstasy had been around much longer but that had been outlawed for years so dealing in it was as risky as coke, puff and smack. It was only when the quality of Ecstasy started to really tumble that all these legal highs began popping up all over the place.

'That's when a mate of mine came to me with a deal which he said could earn me more money than all my earlier drug deals put together. I laughed at him because I couldn't even get my head round the concept of legal highs at that time. For starters they weren't all legal! And they seemed like a complete flash in the pan and a lot of people reckoned they didn't even work properly. Up to then I'd always reckoned they'd soon fade out and no one was likely to make any financial killings from dealing in them because you couldn't really hook punters into them properly.

'But my mate was very persistent and he knew I had a few bob at that time and that I was looking for a decent investment opportunity. So he kept nagging me. In the end I agreed to buy £20,000 worth of mephedrone, which is known to most people as Meow Meow. That was a tester to whet my appetite. My mate got a £2,000 finder's fee and everyone was happy – or so it seemed.

'Unknown to me, my mate had upset a couple of people in the old-fashioned coke trade and they were on the look-out for him over a "debt" concerning a shipment of coke that had gone missing. In fact he was desperately trying to pay them off and that was why he needed the £2k so badly.

'Unaware of all this, I carved up the shipment of Meow Meow and allowed a few of my associates to bounce it around the marketplace. Well, it sold like bleedin' hotcakes and most of my team reported that the majority of customers thought the Meow Meow was cocaine. Now that really got me thinking.

'Then in the middle of all this my original Meow Meow contact got himself shot dead over that drug debt I mentioned earlier. It wasn't that much of a shock because he was always taking the piss and I suspected there'd been a bullet out there with his name on it for a long time. But it was a shame he died because if he'd lived a bit longer he would have made a tidy sum out of my next job.

'After that response to the Meow Meow I decided to take a big punt and buy half a million quid's worth of it from the same source where I got the original, smaller shipment. Well, this fella couldn't believe his ears when I told him. He said it was one of the biggest single shipments ever ordered of the stuff, but I sensed it would be a goldmine, although I knew I'd have to turn the load round very quickly in order to distance myself from it. That's what you always do with a big shipment. The speed it is knocked out at is absolutely essential. The longer it hangs around the more likely someone will hear about it and tell the police.

'And then there was the whole question of quality; I told the supplier that this Meow Meow had to be of the exact same quality as the earlier, smaller shipment. If I thought it was any different I'd demand every penny of my money back. Well, as you can imagine, this guy swore blind it would be exactly the same. I reckoned he wouldn't dare lie to me because I had a bit of a reputation for not suffering fools, if you know what I mean.'

At the same time Mickey was about to buy the biggest-ever single shipment of Meow Meow, the UK tabloids reported the deaths of two people from suspected overdoses of the same substance. 'That was bad news for my marketing men,' explained Mickey. 'The last thing I wanted was a collapse in demand because of a load of scare stories in the red-tops and I was already committed to the shipment.

'Then I had a brainwave. I remembered how my chaps had reported that most customers couldn't tell the difference between Meow Meow and real coke. So I took a big gamble and announced that I'd bought half a million quid's worth of the white stuff, rather than admit it was Meow Meow. Some of my lads knew the truth but I promised them big bonuses if they kept quiet and they began distributing the "cocaine" through their team of street dealers.

'I bought that Meow Meow wholesale for £6 a gram. And my people were knocking out the same stuff for £50 a gram.

I made bleedin' millions. It was like printing money and, you know what? The "cocaine" was sold out inside three weeks and no one seemed bothered. Now a lot of people in my industry would have immediately ploughed some of those profits back into another deal but not me.

'I reckoned I'd never get away with another hit like that, so I stepped back completely from the Meow Meow supplier and the whole business. I let it be known that my missus was very ill and that was the reason. I didn't want anyone to know why I'd really quit because in this game, people get jealous and then they get greedy and dangerous or both.

'I'd made enough money to retire. Sure, I was lucky that none of the punters who'd bought that "coke" worked out it wasn't the real thing. It would have been suicidal to bang out another shipment because then someone would have sussed it out and come after me. I even had a cover story in case there had been any complaints. I was going to say I had no idea and had bought that "coke" in good faith but I never heard a squeak back.'

Today, two years later, Mickey is still sitting on the majority of the fortune he made from that huge Meow Meow shipment. He's been 'extra careful' not to flash all his cash about. He explained: 'Jealous villains and bitty coppers are always a problem, not to mention the bleedin' tax people. I've been careful not to spend all this cash cos that's when loose lips sink ships. About a year after the Meow Meow deal I bought a new house for my family and we eventually splashed out on new cars but not flash ones.

'Then I stopped spending again. The name of the game is to prevent yourself from being flagged up. A mate of mine once fell into the classic trap of splashing out loadsa cash from a big coke deal so openly that he soon got a visit from PC Plod. He ended up serving more time for money laundering than flogging drugs. You have to keep a low profile otherwise it can really cost you.'

Mickey says he enjoys all the luxuries of life 'but in a sensible fashion'. He explained: 'I'm not bigging it up and throwing wads of cash around. I've got a small car repair business and a stake in an old people's home and I manage to clean most of my cash through those legitimate businesses.'

Mickey's own take on the legal-high business hasn't altered one bit. 'Look, I played the game and won. I was lucky in a sense because if I'd bought that big shipment of Meow Meow a few months earlier or later who knows what might have happened. Even villains need a stroke of luck now and again.

'It's funny to think that if it hadn't have been for that bloke who was killed, none of this would have happened and I'd still be ducking and diving around the drug business. He was the one who persuaded me to make that small first purchase and that enabled me to get a toe-hold in the market. That bigger shipment simply cashed in on the trust of customers who'd heard about how good my original product was.'

These days, Mickey insists he is 'as clean as a whistle'. He added: 'I don't need crime any more. I've made my big killing. You know what they say? Everyone needs a pools win in their life to get ahead of the game. Many moons ago an old bank robber I knew said, "Son, if you ever make a fortune out of this game, quit while you're ahead. Don't get greedy cos that's when you'll come tumblin' down and end up in prison or dead. Just get the fuck out of that firing line and thank your lucky stars you've got away with it." '

Mickey went on: 'That was brilliant advice and that old gangster certainly knew a thing or two about crime. You see, it was my own father.'

CHAPTER 12

THADIUS

Thadius seems more like a character out of an Agatha Christie mystery than a serious businessman who claims to have persuaded a bunch of high-end investors to put their money into the legal-high business. Thadius's long sideburns, horn-rimmed glasses and natty tweed suits with brown brogues give the impression he is a country squire but his intention to make tens of millions of pounds out of legal highs is deadly serious.

In 2012, Thadius sat his parents down to tell them about his decision to change careers. Unlike most people in the legal-high trade, he'd decided to come clean with his family. But that didn't stop them being baffled by Thadius's decision to quit his well-paid job in the marketing department of a large British bank to set up a venture capital firm specifically created to invest in the legal-high industry.

Thadius, though, was utterly convinced his instincts were

correct. After years of researching and analysing the financial value of nascent industries, he felt that the legal-high business had the potential to take off in much the same way as electric cars and social media companies and would prove a huge moneyspinner in the long term.

After kicking his outrageous business plan around with three old school friends who were already respected and wealthy venture capitalists, Thadius launched the company, even though he'd have to conceal the true nature of its activities until legal highs were officially licensed. Before then he would have to keep any mention of legal highs away from the spotlight because many of the people involved with the company did not want to be associated with such a questionable business.

Thadius explained: 'Officially, no one would go near legal highs but I knew that if I could get the right level of financial backing then it would eventually all work out fine because in the end the entire business has got to come out in the open.'

Since starting the company, Thadius claims he has received dozens of enquiries from people wanting to invest. 'I've been stunned by how many people recognise it as a big investment opportunity. They're all convinced that certain legal highs will have to be licensed and allowed in all high street shops.'

Thadius revealed many of these potential investors were even prepared to spend part of their money on special labs to help create a legal-high conveyor belt. 'Safety is paramount and once we can convince potential customers that our products are properly tested and completely safe for human consumption then there is no reason why they cannot be sold openly.'

By the summer of 2014, Thadius claimed he had raised £8 million and he intends to raise another £10 million by the end of 2015. 'There is no rush. In some ways it would be more ideal if legal highs were licensed from around 2016 because that gives me plenty of time to get everything in place.

'Listen, it's only a matter of time before the entire business is properly regulated. That's where my company would come in. I see us as being the first ones out there when it's made officially legal. We would clean up. A bit like Coca-Cola did more than a hundred years ago.'

Thadius added that he even planned to employ marketing and public relations experts to help spread the word about legal highs 'when the time is right'.

But he admitted: 'The legal-high business has been stained by some of the dodgy characters in it. Many legal-high entrepreneurs are nothing more than criminals and their priorities lie with replicating illegal drugs like cocaine and then ripping off their customers. That is certainly not my intention. I want this to be a 100 per cent legitimate company when the time is right.'

Thadius admitted, however, that he had already bought up a number of legal-high Internet companies as part of a 'discreet investment schedule'. He explained: 'Just because a company is not actually trading doesn't mean you can't acquire other firms if an opportunity arises and that's exactly what we've been doing. I spotted a couple of legal-high websites that were up for sale, so I snapped them up. It is my intention to buy at least a dozen such companies before we float on the Stock Exchange in 2016.'

Of the two Internet legal-high website companies bought by Thadius's company, one provides an online ratings site for dispensaries and marijuana strains, while the other was producing legal highs for medical purposes.

'These two businesses are perfect for me. I need these smaller firms because I want to build a database of customers and the people who use these sites are very loyal.'

Thadius believes legal highs offer a 'lifestyle choice' to customers mainly under the age of thirty. 'This industry has the potential to sweep up all sorts of other aspects of the life of the under thirties,' he predicted. 'We're not just talking about the legal highs themselves. The sorts of people who take them make certain lifestyle choices and have specific tastes in certain products. This is a commercial goldmine as far as I am concerned. If I can make inroads into that market then this company could become one of the biggest commercial enterprises in the country.'

Thadius has even factored in a possible change of government in the UK into his plans on the basis that a socialist government might be more lenient towards licensing legal highs. 'Labour did that with gambling, didn't they? Don't forget that once this happens then the government will make a fortune in taxes. It's a win-win situation.'

Thadius is convinced that the legal-high industry will in the long term provide 'access to the product and culture. The buyers, the sellers, the takers, they all seem to come out of the same jelly mould and they have plenty of money to spend.'

And like many of the merchants interviewed for this book, Thadius insisted he'd never taken a legal high himself and had no intention of ever doing so. However, he admitted that when he began the business he asked some of his closest friends 'who were into legal highs' to take some of the products he was planning to sell as 'an experiment'. 'They provided me with excellent feedback, which is vital in this industry,' he explained. 'I warned them of the risks from the onset but none of them seemed worried. This is a strange business. People are happy to risk their lives on the say-so of some anonymous chat-room participant.'

Thadius recently hired a former Scotland Yard drugs officer to work on the compliance issues for his company. 'It was vital to have someone with an impeccable reputation on board,' explained Thadius. 'Obviously banks have been cautious about getting involved with my company, fearing they might be charged under drugs racketeering or money-laundering rules. But when I explain the entire business plan in detail they always come round to understanding the potential market for my products and why this company cannot fail in the long term.'

Thadius added: 'I am happy to sit it out for as long as it takes because I recognize that there will always be people who don't want a company like mine to succeed.' He claimed his wide range of investors ranged from 'old hippies to City slickers'. Most prefer to be anonymous. He claimed his investors were 'prepared to be patient and look at the long term'.

He continued: 'I'm not even going to bother trying to market the business outside the UK, US and Europe. These are the most powerful marketplaces without doubt.'

But that's not to say that there isn't money to be made in the Far East: the Japanese in particular are enthusiastically embracing the brave new world of legal highs . . .

CHAPTER 13

TAKI

Taki is responsible for making sure his designer drugs get to thousands of young consumers in Japan's capital city, Tokyo. He admitted he often paid 'top price' for them, some of which are produced in his country but more often they're from abroad. Taki operates from a rented room in the centre of the city, close to the port district where many legal highs are shipped onto the Japanese mainland.

'Many kids want to try them. It's fun and in Japan people have only just begun to discover how to enjoy themselves. You understand? The generation before missed out on illegal drugs because they never really existed here in the same way as so many other parts of the world.'

But Taki is no throwback to the past. He may well act like a Japanese version of Arthur Daley from *Minder* but his clothes were super-trendy and he talked in a gentle voice that included a neat line in sales patter and a strong eye for style. His razor-cut hairstyle certainly made him stand out in the crowd and he's got a disarming level of charm and charisma, which is not always easy to find in Tokyo.

'I love my job,' explained Taki. 'I make much money and everyone is happy. That's the way I want it to always be. Legal highs are *sooooo* Japanese in their concept. The kids here are naturally cautious just like their parents and those parents before them. They are conservative and they don't like taking risks but they feel safer because these drugs are manufactured.

'I think a lot of it is down to the last war when we acted like crazy people and seemed cold and heartless to the rest of the world. But that is not the real Japanese way. We are just very reserved people with steely determination in our blood. We tend to be over-focused and it's only now that we're starting to come out of our shells. Does that make sense?'

But then Taki is not entirely Japanese himself. He says his father was an American diplomat who met his mother in Tokyo. 'That in itself was a shaming situation back when I was born in the late seventies,' says Taki. 'No one likes to talk about such relationships. You see, Japanese people like to think of themselves as pure both racially and intellectually.'

Taki is mightily proud of his job as one of Tokyo's busiest legal-high suppliers. He described the background for me: 'When I first started in this business six years ago, everyone was scared of all drugs, the stuff you buy on the street and the stuff you could get on the Internet. But then I went to Europe on vacation one time and met some old friends and we got high on some herbal hash. I knew straight away this sort of stuff would really appeal to Japanese kids.

'Obviously I appreciate the psyche of Japanese youth. They are desperate to break away from the same mundane lives that their parents led and do wild stuff. Get high, drink alcohol, chase girls, maybe even have some casual relationships. But you must remember that it's all still relatively new to Japanese kids. Anyhow, when I got back to Japan from that vacation in Europe, I decided to research legal highs very carefully on the Internet.

'I spent months ordering small samples and trying them. I also started to test them out on my friends to see what they thought of them and we soon established which ones worked and which ones were useless!'

But again the Japanese psyche is important to consider here. As Taki explained: 'Young people here don't want to break the law just so they can enjoy themselves. It's not the same as in the West where people seem to break the law much more often. If a Japanese kid gets arrested for taking illegal drugs it brings deep shame on his family and that is too much responsibility for most Japanese children to handle. But the introduction of legal highs has been like a dream come true for a lot of Japanese kids.

'Anyways, back to my story. So I spent some months testing out many different kinds of legal highs, which I bought from the Internet. They were very different in quality and it soon became apparent to me that the suppliers were key to the quality issues. I noticed that often when I purchased legal highs direct from companies in China and India the substances were very weak and in many cases did not work at all. It was clear that this was the biggest weakness in the system. It meant that people ordering legal highs directly online were finding themselves often disappointed and that made them not trust the suppliers. My job was to make sure they came back for more.

'In Tokyo I came across some people who'd tried legal highs and they had been through the same experience, which had resulted in them not trusting the Internet. They told me they were so disappointed that often they just stopped buying legal highs altogether, even though they remained interested in taking them *if* they really worked. Well, that was when I recognized the hole in the market and how there was a role for me in this.

'First I began by going back to the suppliers of the better quality legal highs, who tended to come from the UK and Europe. I discovered from talking to them that they sourced their drugs from very specific factories, where they knew the quality of the produce was superior. But they were not happy to tell me the names of those factories, so I did some more detailed research and found out for myself. Then I started to order in quite large quantities from those same suppliers.

'Then I set up online and opened a store in a busy suburb at the same time. It was the equivalent of a head shop in England, I guess. You know the funny thing? More people started coming into my store than were buying my stuff from the Internet. You see, these people felt more trusting of what they were buying when they came into my store and talked in detail about what they wanted. I would chat about all the different products as they told me what they wanted to feel from taking the legal highs. Often myself or my assistant would spend maybe as much as thirty minutes talking to people before they bought anything but it was worth it because they soon started coming back every week to buy more.'

Taki made no attempt to keep his business underground as none of the drugs he was selling were illegal under Japanese law at the time. 'Hey, I was running a legitimate business, so why should I hide? But I was stupid in many ways because I did not allow for the backlash from the parents of many of these kids who came to my store. They looked on me as some kind of devil in disguise, selling their children evil substances that might end up turning them into drug addicts.

'That was a difficult time for me. I felt I was doing nothing wrong but these parents wanted to kill off my business. There I was, providing a much needed "filter" for these kids to get their own supplies of legal highs safe in the knowledge that I had tested them and knew they would actually work. But the parents did not look at it in that way. One time I tried to explain this to two angry fathers who came into my store armed with baseball bats and determined to smash it to bits. I said to them that without me their kids would have been ordering stuff online without knowing anything about what those drugs contained. They looked at me like I was insane at first but gradually they calmed down and we had a proper conversation and they started to understand my role.

'I explained it to them like this: what would they prefer? That their children tried to score illegal drugs on street corners or ordered so-called legal highs off the Internet, which could then kill them? At least, I said to them, I'm here providing some kind of safety valve for the kids. You know what? In the end they agreed not to return to my store.'

But not all parents were so forgiving of Taki, who by this time was known as 'Mister Legal High' in the neighbourhood. He explained: 'Sure, there were other parents who could not be persuaded and I guess it was kind of inevitable that eventually they would try and force the police to shut down my store. I found this very frustrating as well as being extremely short sighted.'

On more than half a dozen occasions, groups of angry parents attacked Taki in the street. He explained: 'A lot of my customers were too scared to come in my store because their parents were picketing outside. The police were not very helpful, either. They obviously disapproved of what I was doing and although they could not close the store down, they made it clear they wanted me to leave. The final straw came when I was approached by the father of one of my customers, who turned out to be the chief of the local police. I knew then it was time to make a break before I ended up in jail.'

Taki then closed his corner store in the suburbs and set up a legal-high supply chain from a couple of rented rooms near Tokyo's bustling port. He explained: 'I had a good reputation by this time and I didn't see why I should just quit but I realized that I needed to keep a much lower profile. Many of my original customers promised me they would continue to use me even after I closed my store.'

That was in 2012. Since then, Taki said his business had continued to boom more than ever before. 'The funny thing is that by moving into these offices near the port I have found even more customers. They seem to prefer to come here to get their supplies rather than go into a proper store in their own neighbourhood. I guess I was asking for trouble opening that store in the first place. These kids want to get high without their parents knowing and I was kind of advertising it all in their faces, so it's no wonder I got such a backlash.'

Taki has now expanded his business by buying in new strands of legal highs specifically produced inside Japan. 'It's a crazy situation but some kids are starting to develop their own legal highs for a fraction of what they pay for my products. Rather than compete with them, I encouraged them to send me some samples so I could test their stuff out. If it is good and safe then I will recommend it. I like doing this even though it encourages home-produced legal highs. I know they are cheaper but I still retain the same profit margin and the Japanese much prefer to use products manufactured here rather than abroad.'

Taki claimed he had thousands of customers on his database. 'Business is good. There are more drug choices out there to confuse people so I have become like this expert who is trusted to recommend stuff that people feel safe to use.'

Taki now even puts his own stamp of approval on every packet that he recommends. 'People seem to feel more secure if Taki has "passed" the product. It goes back to that word of mouth thing that is so important in any personalized business.'

Taki told me that since the end of 2013 he had imported less than 50 per cent of his goods from outside Japan. 'It's a booming market here. When I first started out there were no home-based producers of legal highs. Now it is getting more and more prevalent. I much prefer dealing with Japanese people for these products. I trust them more and I know they're very responsible when it comes to the ingredients. They're also very precise and they are obsessed with making sure each sachet or pill has exactly the same amount of ingredients in it. A lot of the legal highs I bought abroad in the early days were very randomly produced and, quite frankly, it was impossible to know what was really in each product.

'People need to understand that the only reason people get sick from taking legal highs is because the products are put together very casually. Here in Japan it is just not the way we operate.'

Taki predicts that within five years, all legal highs on sale in Japan will be manufactured domestically. 'It makes sense. I have no problem with quality control. In fact, I hope the government gets more proactive in that area because then more Japanese will take legal highs and I will get richer!'

He added: 'People need to realize that carefully produced legal highs are a fantastic alternative to illegal drugs if they're allowed to develop as a proper industry. People will always want to get high, so what's the problem with giving them something safe and legal rather than deadly? Think about it.'

Taki was lucky enough to be able to tap into a market right on his doorstep, but there are others in the legal-high game who've had to travel further afield to make sure they get their slice of the action.

CHAPTER 14

JERRY

Jerry describes himself as an 'opportunist', originally from Florida, who claims he's already sold almost a million dollars' worth of legal highs from his 'headquarters' in Brazil.

'I like to think of myself as an entrepreneur,' said Jerry. 'If it hadn't been legal highs then it might well have been automobile parts or coat hangers. I'm interested in the art of the sale more than the specific product. But I make sure my legal highs are of the highest quality.'

Jerry, now in his mid-forties, admits he's had a checkered working career. 'I've been a manager of a candy factory, a chauffeur for a rich guy, a bus driver for school kids. But the one thing I've always retained is a work ethic. I've tried starting up a lot of businesses down the years because I've always believed in myself and my ability to succeed. Even when none of those businesses got off the ground, it felt like I was in training to make money and I knew that one day I'd get a lucky break.'

That 'lucky break' came when a cousin of Jerry's cornered him at a family party in Florida and began singing the praises of legal highs. 'I didn't know what the kid was on about at first,' recalled Jerry. 'To be honest about it, I thought he was off his head on drugs! He kept telling me that legal highs would make me a fortune and that I'd be a fool not to get into the business before the whole world turned on to them.

'He told me how many of his old school friends took them and how they were relatively harmless but they were much more popular than illegal drugs. He even reckoned they were safer. I'd never been into drugs in my life, so it was difficult at first to appreciate his point of view. But then he began telling me how much they cost to make and what they were selling for on the Internet.

'I tell you, my ears pricked up and I smelled a deal there and then. My cousin said that a lot of kids were ordering inferior drugs online and he was convinced that suppliers were ripping off their customers bigtime. That got me thinking about the customer base and how I could provide a service that might be able to guarantee them the real thing, rather than a tablet full of baking soda.

'First of all, I employed my cousin to do a sweep of the Internet and get samples of everything that was available, so we could assess what the best products were. I left it to him and his friends to test them all out. But then we hit a problem. No sooner had they tried out the products then the best-selling ones got outlawed.

'So I went to see a lawyer friend of mine to try and work out if there was a way round this because it would be a disaster if I ordered a huge shipment of one product and then it became outlawed before I even had a chance to sell it. My attorney friend said the only way round it was for me to base myself in another country that wouldn't quickly ban them.

'At first I thought there was no real point in carrying on. It was just gonna end up being yet another business that I couldn't get off the ground. Then fate took a hand in it all. I'd been dating this girl for years and we were about to announce plans to marry and she went and ran off with one of my best friends.

'That kinda sealed my decision to try and get into the legal-high deal business. What was the point in staying in the US? Every corner I turned in my hometown, I came face to face with reminders of my ex-girlfriend and some of my family members even took her side and said she did it because I didn't move fast enough to marry her in the first place. It was a terrible time for me emotionally. I just wanted to escape from there and never come back.

'That got me thinking back to what my lawyer friend had told me about moving abroad and I realized it was a case of now or never. So I took the plunge and headed out to Brazil. Why Brazil? Well, if I'm to be completely honest about it, I liked the look of the women down there and I heard you could live there real cheaply. I didn't have much money and

I wanted to keep most of it to pay for the start-up costs for my business. Brazil ticked all the right boxes for me.'

So, armed with a couple of thousand dollars, Jerry headed to São Paulo, the biggest city in the southern hemisphere. He admitted: 'It was a complete shot in the dark and one hell of a culture shock. I didn't know anyone. I didn't speak Portuguese. I was just a dumbass jock from Florida. Looking back on it, I was pretty dumb to think I could manage to survive in a place like SP, but then again sometimes in life you gotta take those sorta risks.

'So I got myself a cheap apartment. I went online and began ordering in all the legal highs that my cousin said were good quality. Then I got him and his friends back in Florida to start reviewing them online and giving my company a plug at the same time. I promised to pay them 10 per cent of my revenue as a fee.'

Within six weeks of arriving in Brazil, Jerry says his apartment was filled to the brim with boxes of legal highs, most of which had been shipped in from China and India. 'You could hardly walk in the door I had so much of the stuff. At one stage I had to create a corridor between the boxes so I could get to the bathroom and the kitchen.

'But the cool thing about going somewhere completely new is that you can start your life again. Nobody sticks their nose in your business. You don't have all the same distractions as you have at home. I was completely focused on my business and I worked virtually 24/7 to get it up and running.'

Jerry said that his neighbours in the apartment block where he lived were soon 'mightily confused' by his activities. 'Out here they just presume you're a drug dealer if you make any big money and run your business from home. And in many ways I used that impression to my advantage. People left me alone because they thought I must be a dangerous criminal. I didn't deny it because I didn't want any people trying to muscle in on my business.'

Jerry recalled that during that first year in Brazil, he built up the turnover of his legal-high business to $10,000 a month. 'I got on a roll real quick,' he remembered. 'I had a good system going and my suppliers never sent me inferior product because they knew I'd just go to someone else if they tried to rip me off.'

By basing his business in Brazil, Jerry discovered he was not breaking any of the US's strict sub-laws about the supply and sale of legal highs. 'Back in the States, they consider guys like me to be as bad as illegal drug dealers. But even more worrying than that, the tax people at the IRS always demand a big chunk of your income and I didn't want that type of hassle either.'

Now – three years later – Jerry's legal-high business is thriving but like so many in this business he insisted on complete secrecy about his real identity and the specific location of his business. He explained: 'I don't want to rub anyone's nose in it. I don't want folks to know what I do, for all sorts of obvious reasons.

'The biggest reason is that here in Brazil, there are a lot of dangerous desperados who'd probably slit my throat and take over my business if they knew how much money I was making. I earn a fortune by their standards and I've seen other businesses taken over by gangsters in this city. It's a ruthless place. Lives are cheap out here.

'There is also a lot of resentment against Americans in general. We're seen as rich even when we are not and in fairness to most of the people here, they are extremely poor and treated like dirt by the super-wealthy five per cent of the population. I always tell people I'm Canadian when they ask me because I know how much hatred there is here against Americans.

'The other big reason I like to keep it all low-key and discreet is that currently the US doesn't have the resources to deal with guys like me working on the edge of the legal-high business. They'll leave me alone just so long as I don't operate inside the States.

'I know from my friends at the American consulate here that the Brazilian government would never agree to extradite me just because I was involved in the legal-high business. Back in the US, I'd have to have all sorts of licences to operate and all my products would have to be given full governmental approval. Obviously that is not possible with legal highs. I'd never be able to operate my business if I had to stick to those US rules. I had no choice but to come out here.'

However, Jerry knows full well that if his business continues to grow at the rate it currently is, then one day he'll get a visit from the Brazilian authorities. 'At the moment, I'm just a hard-working trader in their eyes and I'm bringing money into Brazil so they leave me in peace. But some greedy cop will knock on my door one day and then I guess I'll have to pay him off.'

Jerry is so careful he still rents the same small apartment he moved into when he first arrived in São Paulo, even though he goes home every evening to a large detached house in an upmarket suburb. 'Very few people here know that I have another home. They just presume I live in this small rental but that's the way I like it. I don't drive an expensive automobile and even when I date local women, I'm extremely careful not to tell them the nature of my business, although some of them are very nice to me because they just presume I am a rich gringo.

'When they're like that, I always bring them back to my crap little apartment to make them think I don't have any money! It's worked very well most of the time. I like the feeling that few people know what I do. It gives me a sense of freedom and security.'

Jerry said he had learned 'the hard way' to be extremely careful when dating local women. 'When I first got here I was like a kid in a candy store. They all looked real beautiful and sexy and I couldn't take my eyes off them and they started swarming around me like bees to a honeypot. I went kinda crazy for a while.

'Then I settled down and started seriously dating. I had a relationship with this woman who seemed real nice at first.

She spoke perfect English, which is unusual out here, and we spent weekends together on the beach and stuff like that.

'I began to wonder if maybe she was the one for me in the long term. But then one day I was having dinner with her in a restaurant near my small apartment and there was this guy sitting near us whom she obviously knew. I caught her smiling and nodding at him. Well, I took one look at all the gold he was wearing and his jailhouse tattoos and worked out he was some kind of local gangster. He even had a diamond stud in his teeth.

'Then I got to thinking that maybe she'd been trying to lure me into some kind of honey trap so this guy could take over my business. It's sad to be so suspicious but that's how things work out here. So I did a bit of snooping of my own and discovered she was actually living with this gangster guy all the time she'd been going out with me. That was like a very big warning sign to be careful.

'I was lucky. I managed to end the relationship without her realizing I knew about her boyfriend. I don't know why to this day they didn't just raid my apartment and try to steal all my product. All I can presume is that I ended the relationship before they could work out exactly what I was doing in São Paulo.'

And throughout his stay in Brazil, Jerry claimed he'd never once been tempted to take illegal or legal drugs, or to sell his own product on his doorstep. 'You would not believe how many drugs are easily available out here,' he exclaimed. 'I know there is a ready-made market for legal highs but if

I started stealing customers from any gangsters, I'd soon find myself dead.

'In any case, they just can't comprehend the concept of legal highs. Brazilian society seems to thrive on the poor people being stoned on illicit drugs most of the time. It effectively freezes these people. They can't move forward because the drugs have addled their brains. It's very sad but this is a twisted society in so many ways.

'Drugs like crack cocaine are so popular that the income derived from it gives employment to many people, as well as providing street dealers and their families with enough money to spend at local stores and other businesses. Drugs are part of the financial infrastructure out here. If you took away the illegal drugs there would be a civil war within weeks.'

Jerry claimed that in the summer of 2013, he was approached by the US consulate in São Paulo. 'I knew some folk on the social circuit over there so I agreed to go into a meeting with their commercial attaché on the basis that they couldn't touch me over here. Trouble was that they then introduced me to the Brazilian rep for the DEA [US Drug Enforcement Administration]!'

Jerry continued: 'They wanted me to help them source out some of the suppliers of the more dangerous legal highs and offered me immunity from prosecution in exchange for my help. I was outraged. It felt like they were bullying me but I knew they couldn't touch me in Brazil, so I challenged them by refusing to help.

'They threatened all sorts of stuff but none of it ever came to anything and they couldn't do a damn thing to stop me running my business. They even informed the Brazilian tax people about my activities but when I spoke to them they laughed and said they had no interest in me whatsoever. The whole experience left me realizing you just can't trust anyone. The DEA were nasty and underhand and it left a bad taste in my mouth. They had no right to try to blackmail me like that.'

Jerry said that the experience left him convinced he should never return to live in the US. 'I'd harboured dreams of going back to Florida one day but now I reckon I am better off here in Brazil.'

Meanwhile Jerry continues to run his business 'under the radar'. He went on: 'It's the perfect environment for me. I'm not taking any of these people's income from illegal drugs away from them. I'm simply running an outlet store for legal highs to be sent to customers all over the world. I guess I could have done this from many other places but Brazil just happens to be where I've ended up.'

Jerry revealed he was now involved in a 'real relationship' with an American woman he met through the Internet. 'She's been over to see me here and the long-term plan is for her to join me here full time eventually. She knows what I do for a living and she has no problem with it. But then why should she? I'm doing nothing actually illegal. We hope to get married soon. She's an open-minded person like me and she also has a sense of adventure. This business has enabled

me to feel as if I'm having a real life adventure that hopefully will never end.'

While Jerry took a while to realize that his true calling
was as a legal-high entrepreneur, there are some bright
sparks out there who have got going before they've even left
school.

CHAPTER 15

MATT AND NEIL

Legal highs are rapidly growing in popularity in schools because of their easy accessibility and because many youngsters think they're safer than illegal drugs. So when two young 'entrepreneurs' called Matt and Neil noticed that a lot of their contemporaries at the sixth form of a public school in the UK were constantly talking about their wish to experiment with legal highs, they spotted 'a unique business opportunity'.

Explained Matt: 'From what I'd heard, the old-time illegal drug business was very hard to get into unless you had the contacts but legal highs are easy to access on the Internet, so my mate Neil and I decided to launch our first business by supplying them.'

Interrupted Neil: 'Even more importantly, we reckoned we wouldn't even get expelled if we were caught because, after all, they are legal highs.'

And the two sharp-eyed teenagers were proved absolutely right.

Matt continued: 'We tested the school reaction by being deliberately caught with a couple of packets of legal highs. It was exactly as we thought. We got ticked off but nothing more. What can they do when they find you with stuff you can openly buy on the Internet or through a head shop?'

Within weeks, Matt and Neil had set up their own supply chain and were selling products to classmates and others in the school, as well as through friends at other schools. 'It took off because a lot of kids were scared stiff of buying this stuff off the Internet or from a bloke in a pub. They liked the fact they knew us. It also convinced them that the quality of the product will be half decent because we wouldn't be selling it to them if it wasn't.'

One of the most popular legal highs they sold was nicknamed 'Bubble' or 'Drone', and had a similar effect to Ecstasy. 'Everyone's always having parties at each other's homes and this stuff is perfect and much harder to detect than alcohol, so parents don't have a clue about it,' said Neil.

Matt explained: 'Legal highs are good news for us but a nightmare for the schools. After we got caught deliberately that first time our school got the head of chemistry to explain to all the sixth formers about the dangers of legal highs during a special assembly. It felt like too little too late to us and actually a lot of our friends found it very informative for when they next bought legal highs off us.'

Matt and Neil say that teenagers like them and their class-mates are the main target market for legal highs. 'We take our duty of care very seriously and always look to educate our friends about the dangers of drug use before they buy anything from us. But ultimately, it's a free world and kids like us love to experiment.'

When I interviewed Matt and Neil they were about to start their last round of school exams and even claimed that some students were buying legal highs from them in order to stay awake while revising. 'Having that market cornered has helped make us a load more money. I've even started recommending certain products for that purpose and it does help, although I am not sure if it helps the memory!'

Both teenagers said they aimed to 'retire' once they left school, although they also admitted they'd looked at the possibility of running similar 'chains' when they got to uni-versity. 'But ultimately we look on this as part of "training" for the big wide world.'

However, Matt and Neil are by no means the only school-age legal-high entrepreneurs . . .

In Liverpool, police believe many teenage schoolchildren are 'playing Russian roulette' by selling and taking locally produced legal highs. This city in the north of England has long been a notorious entry point for the smuggling of cocaine but this new development regarding legal highs has taken local law enforcement completely by surprise.

Enter Kally and Ed: they've just left school at the

minimum age of sixteen and are already running a lucrative operation, selling mainly to schoolchildren. Kally explained: 'It's better for them to take this stuff than coke, ain't it?'

When I pointed out that it was not necessarily the case, they looked blankly back at me.

'We get kids as young as twelve wanting legal highs and so we try to have a rule not to sell to youngsters, but it's hard to work out the age of many kids these days,' said Ed. 'Listen, everyone round here takes something, so it might as well be the legal stuff, eh? Also, the real gangsters in these parts are all into coke dealing. They ain't worked out this market yet so there's plenty of money to be made.'

Kally and Ed act as if their legal highs are as harmless as Smarties in a sweet shop but the reality is that in Liverpool a wave of locally produced legal highs have been hitting the streets in recent years and many experts believe they are often more lethal than crack, heroin and cocaine.

Only a few weeks before I met Kally and Ed, four pupils at one Liverpool school had to be taken to hospital after smoking a synthetic version of cannabis on a school playing field. One boy, aged just fourteen, suffered a seizure and three other youngsters were left vomiting after inhaling herbal incense at another school. They'd taken a drug designed to mimic the effects of cannabis that was in packaging marked 'not for human consumption'.

Kally explained: 'We were very sorry to hear about what happened to those kids but that had nothing to do with us. We don't even go near either of those schools. We know that many kids take legal highs because they like to think they are illegal drugs and it makes them feel more grown up. We're just meeting that demand.'

Both boys refused to say who supplied them with the drugs they sold or where they got the money from in the first place to launch their 'business'.

One local drug counsellor said: 'The legal-high dealers round here are a very mixed bunch. They're often people who've previously dealt in illegal drugs and have moved on to what they think is legal stuff because it's easier to get hold of and they can make a bigger mark-up. Others are just kids trying to make some extra pocket money. A lot of the time they approach people and give it to them for free and then they "lay it down" for them so that they always have a debt. Quite often some youngsters go into dealing themselves to pay off that debt.'

Kally and Ed said that a lot of the children they sold legal highs to actually took them inside their schools. 'I know one kid who pops something every single day. He says it makes school much easier to handle. I wish I'd tried some meself when I was at school. The way we look at it is that these kids are just havin' a laugh. It's not harmin' anyone, is it?'

The same Liverpool drug counsellor added: 'They might think it's a laugh but these legal-high drugs are very danger-ous. They contain chemicals that can kill and maim people. The main thing we need to do is try and give these kids some preventative education. We can't completely stop people taking drugs. If people want to take drugs, they will go out and find them. But we want to make sure they are making an informed choice.'

Back in London, Dev, eighty-one, has been a drug baron for more than forty years and openly admits he often snorts more cocaine than he sells, breaking the golden drug-dealing rule – don't get high on your own supply. But these days, his drug of choice is mephedrone, which he prefers to call Meow Meow. Now in semi-retirement and living in an old people's home, Dev started off selling Meow Meow to a close-knit circle of old criminal associates and friends to 'make a few extra bob'.

Dev is convinced that substitutes for cocaine will 'eventually take over the coke market completely'. In his darkened care-home flat, Dev weighs up the Meow Meow that he always packs in special plastic twist baggies that are his unique calling card. He claims he now has customers who include some members of London's elite media set and 'even a couple of VIPs'.

Dev insists he openly admits the real nature of what he is selling to his customers. 'It's better this way then there's no comeback. I tell them all it's as good as coke and they genuinely believe me. I sell grams and eight balls – which is basically an eighth of an ounce. My customers all come here to get it. Much safer than going out into the big bad world and risking a pull from the long arm of the law.'

Dev spends most of his time inside his cramped flat watching the cricket and the football on Sky TV. He says he likes the high from Meow Meow more than the hyper feeling that cocaine used to provide.

'It's gentler and more mellow but it works just as well,' says Dev. 'Whenever my mates ask me about it I always put it like this: what would you prefer to take? Something that's been stamped on by some smelly, sweaty feet in a Colombian jungle or something that's been carefully manufactured in a pristine factory in the middle of China? It's a great sales pitch, isn't it?'

Dev has London and south-east England criminal connections going back more than sixty years and he argues that drugs changed the face of crime for ever. He explained: 'I try not to look backwards to the old days but there was a time when any drugs were considered the devil's candy. People who took them were burnt-out losers and the underworld looked down on the users.

'But then cocaine appeared on the scene and it seemed to pep people up and some even claimed it helped them work better. It was only after that that the old-school villains moved into the drugs trade but none of us could have predicted that drugs would be manufactured legally and sold as such.

'The government is stupid because if they had any sense they'd make it all above board and then tax it to shit and add billions to their coffers. But there's still a lot of fear and trepidation even about legal highs, as well as old-time illegal drugs. I won't be around for much longer but I'm sure there will come a day when drugs are available across every counter. God knows what all the villains will get up to then!'

Dev has a fascinating theory as to why his customers are happy to buy Meow Meow from him rather than cocaine. 'They love pretending it's the real stuff,' he suggested. 'It makes them feel more daring and in their eyes I'm the Mister Big of the drug-dealing trade. It's a bit of a joke, really, but then who am I to complain? Most of these characters have lived their lives ducking and diving and even in old age they like to think they're getting up to no good.'

But what sets the legal-high industry apart from the old-fashioned trade in illicit narcotics is that gradually it is attracting more and more legitimate business people convinced that they are simply supplying a demand.

PART THREE

TRANSPORTERS/DEALERS –
USA, SPAIN, UK, HOLLAND

A study by the Global Drug Survey found that the UK has the highest proportion of legal-high users in the world. One in ten of the 7,000 Brits polled admitted taking legal-high substances. That's double the global average.

CHAPTER 16

LOU

Lou, forty-three, from Newcastle had always struggled to keep his import/export business afloat. He'd just about managed to keep his head above water when the onset of the depression in 2008 fired a torpedo at his company's chances of survival. Debts piled up. The bank came knocking and Lou found himself desperately looking round for new business opportunities. Today, he claims he had no choice but to enter the shadowy world of legal highs. He had spotted what he calls a 'hole in the market'.

Lou openly admitted he'd dabbled with recreational drugs most of his adult life and that fuelled his interest in entering the 'business'. Initially, he focused in on mephedrone as it closely resembled cocaine, his personal narcotic of choice. But when mephedrone was banned in most Western countries in 2010, Lou joined forces with a chemistry-savvy partner and they developed a cocaine-like legal high which was devised by tweaking the molecular structure of a well-known prescription drug.

'It is the bee's knees,' claimed Lou, who currently lives 'somewhere in Holland'. He and his 'sleeping partner' are classic examples of the type of European-based entrepreneurs who are currently cashing in on legal highs.

'We're taking on the big boys,' said Lou. 'People like me are trying to make money from drugs legally. It's not easy, I can tell you.'

Lou uses his own version of business logic to explain the commercial advantages of his new career: 'The global epicentre for legal highs is centred around Europe, so it makes complete sense to be based here. People in Europe are much more used to buying drugs online as well, which helps. Europe is like this giant first-time testing marketplace. If certain legal highs sell well here then you can be pretty sure they will go down a storm elsewhere in the world.'

Lou describes himself as 'nothing more than a salesman' and says he visits the lucrative wholesale market constantly trying to drum up big orders for his products. And if he can secure those orders, he knows he can rake it in. As Lou confided: 'It's simple. The mark-up on my products is almost twice that of illegal drugs such as cocaine.'

But he also exposed his own cynical attitude when it came to the dangers of taking legal highs he has supplied. 'Saying on the label "not fit for human consumption" ensures no one can sue me,' Lou asserted. 'That phrase gives me airtight protection. In any case, the police have got enough on their hands policing the kind of blokes that are bringing kilos of smack into the country. Why would they bother with a guy like me?'

Lou also insisted that all his products were 'extremely carefully' tested. And it was in this particular respect that Lou differed from the other men involved in this business that I met while researching this book. He explained: 'There is a group of us who regularly take our products to make sure they are okay. I love this part because I genuinely enjoy taking drugs. Sometimes we sit with a pen and paper, and note down all the reactions. Other times if it's more of a party product we go out clubbing and see how it reacts.'

Lou may consider himself a legitimate, hard-working businessman but that wasn't enough to stop Dutch Customs officials who recently raided one of his storehouses and seized a quantity of his chemicals. As it stands they have to use obscure legislation designed to regulate other substances to justify their actions, but Lou knows it's only a matter of time before his work is subject to more comprehensive and forceful scrutiny from the law. Lou's short-term answer is to move to one of the former Eastern Bloc countries 'because they don't interfere on this level'.

Lou explained: 'I just look on that sort of stuff as inconvenient but nothing more. It doesn't stop me operating. I've got eight employees and a lot of product to shift every week. Business is great. Eventually, I'd like to set up shop back in Newcastle but for now Eastern Europe is the place to head for.'

Lou and his sleeping partner are constantly tweaking the ingredients of his cocaine-like product to ensure that it avoids being made illegal. He continued: 'I've got a good system in place. I produce just enough each month and as we get closer to the end of a window, I wind down production of whatever products I think will be banned and start to work on new, legal versions.'

In anticipation of these official banning orders, Lou admitted he was developing other legal-high products, including a number of drugs that resembled Ecstasy. He went on: 'That's what most people in this business are aiming for. The five-star gold product which sells in tens of thousands of units for a few months until it gets banned, making people like me extremely rich. I haven't got there yet but that is my ultimate ambition.' His team are constantly online looking for new legal highs to develop. 'Research is the key to what I do. You need to keep one step ahead of the authorities and at the same time ensure that your product will connect with legal-high users. It's a precarious balancing act at times.'

Lou openly admits he would steal ideas for new legal highs from the Internet – both plagiarizing scientific papers and tracking message boards to see what the psychonauts are currently buzzing about. His ultimate aim, he says, is to produce a vast range of new products. He explained: 'Competition is fierce and often the first one to spot something online is the one who makes a real killing. It's dog eat dog out there.' As a result of this Lou explained that he tries to keep his business 'very low-key'. 'I don't want to even discuss the equipment we use to turn a lot of our products into powder because it might give away our "production techniques" to our rivals.' He's also wary of drawing too much unwanted attention on himself from the authorities.

'Sure, I'm careful,' said Lou. 'I don't want to rub anyone's nose in it. I want my business to thrive, not be closed down, so I keep it all low-key and long may it stay that way.' But avoiding trouble doesn't mean abandoning his ambitions for the business.

Lou believes that his company will 'go from strength to strength'. He went on: 'I'm a great believer in branding and I'm trying to subtly use my products and my company name to promote a cool image, so that gradually I can move into other products apart from legal highs. That means that I won't be so reliant on just legal highs for my income so that if they're outlawed I've got a healthy spin-off business to help it all tick along nicely.'

CHAPTER 17

GEOFF

Geoff, in his mid-thirties, is already a relatively old hand in the legal-high game. He owns a small warehouse/barn in Devon, from which he distributes every kind of legal high available on the market through his cleverly designed websites. He refused to confirm or deny whether all his products were tested but claimed he'd never had any complaints from his tens of thousands of customers across the world.

Like so many of those working in the legal-high underworld, Geoff refused to allow himself or the location of his storage unit to be identified because he genuinely feared that professional criminals might try and take over his business once they became aware of the vast profits involved. 'I know I'm making a much bigger mark-up than, say, a coke dealer in London and eventually the villains will try and get a piece of this but hopefully I will have made my fortune by then and got out of this game.'

Geoff – who described himself as 'an old hippy at heart' – explained how he 'stumbled into' the legal-high business. 'I spent most of my twenties rolling around the UK festival circuit, running food stands and scraping a living together. In the winter, I made most of my income from car boot sales. It was a hand-to-mouth existence in many ways but I liked the freedom of being on the road.

'I converted an old ambulance into a mobile food stand and I prided myself on the quality of my produce and tried to be as creative as possible with the sort of dishes I provided. Then I got into location catering for the film and TV business and started working flat out on films and TV dramas. The money was amazingly good but it was incredibly hard work and I soon burned out. It's no picnic, feeding fifty fussy, spoilt film cast and crew starting at five a.m. and ending at midnight most days. No wonder I burned out.

'Then my wife left me for my best friend and took our five children with her. I was left with nothing. The house we owned was heavily mortgaged and I had to sell it to pay her her share, so when the divorce came through I was left with pretty much nothing but a few thousand pounds.

'So I bought myself an old campervan and started living in it wherever I felt like stopping. It was a pretty unhealthy existence. I tried to continue film work but I was so torn apart by the end of my marriage that I started not turning up for film shoots and eventually I got such a bad name the work just dried up.

'That's when I stumbled on some legal highs at a festival in the West Country. It was a pretty exclusive event, only about five thousand people were invited, all through word of mouth. It was a closed environment hosted by some titled family and all sorts of illegal and legal drugs were openly available. People were taking stuff like laughing gas out in the open. It was eye-opening because for the first time I realized there was a whole drug netherworld out there that I knew nothing about. I'd been a big hash smoker up till then but hardly ever took anything else.

'Anyway, I got talking to these guys who were selling legal highs and it struck me that within a few years these sorts of products would be more easily available than illegal drugs. And most importantly, these legal highs were dirt cheap so they were capable of providing big profits if marketed the right way.'

So Geoff decided to look more closely at the trade in these new psychotropics. 'I was in need of a steady income from something that didn't involve travelling round the country the whole time,' he explained. 'I was hardly ever seeing my kids and I needed some stability in my life. I found a massive empty barn in Devon, rented it for a song from a local farmer and set myself up in the legal-high business.

'Obviously it wasn't easy at first. Just like any business, you have to find the reliable suppliers, you have to negotiate the best wholesale prices and you have to trust those suppliers to provide you with proper, genuine product. But I enjoyed the challenge of it all. My overheads were incredibly low in the early days. I didn't tell the farmer but I used to sleep in one corner of that barn to save myself the rent on a proper home. I think he knew I was overnighting, but we got on very well so it didn't really bother him.

'Anyway, that allowed me to set up the business without going broke before it had taken off. It's very important to have that sort of cushion to give yourself a chance to make a mark. No business takes off overnight. You have to make it work and that takes time.'

Geoff said he had a golden rule *not* to take any of the legal highs he sells. 'I had a bad experience with some MDMA when I was on the festival circuit a few years back, so I swore off taking anything after that. But I knew what it was like to get high and I knew there were a lot of people out there who'd like to do that very thing, but in a controlled environment instead of buying some old crap off a bloke in a pub.'

Geoff admitted that for the first year after setting up his business, he struggled to make ends meet. 'I'd started from scratch. I needed to build my contacts and most importantly I needed the outlets for my produce. The produce itself was at rock bottom price back then [2009] so I was able to stockpile a lot of it in the barn.

'The other great thing about legal highs is there are few sell-by dates. That means you can store them for ages and they're all in carefully sealed packaging so there are no problems with damp and conditions. That was a real bonus to me back then because the barn was cold and draughty!'

The low cost of those legal highs promised Geoff an incredibly high mark-up if he could find the right outlets. He explained: 'So I started driving round the country visiting all the head shops and offering my products for sale. It was a bit like being a door-to-door salesman but with one very big difference. My potential customers were incredibly receptive. I discovered that hardly anyone ever bothered to visit these shops and they were effectively ordering blind from their suppliers, who were often abroad, and they were being regularly ripped off.'

After just one complete round-Britain trip, Geoff started to get big orders. 'Immediately after that things began to really take off. The shops loved the fact I was English and based in Devon rather than some strange place they couldn't even pronounce the name of. I was also managing to get the products for such low prices that I wasn't charging any more than they were already paying for dodgy legal-high products from abroad.'

Within a year, Geoff claims he was supplying 30 per cent of all the head shops in Britain and Ireland. 'But I have to admit there weren't that many back then so I recognized that I needed to put my expertise onto the Internet as well. So I set up an online legal-high supply store but I was extremely careful not to undercut the legal-high shops, who were my main customers.

'They were incredibly appreciative of that fact and it

helped build an even bigger bond of trust between myself and the shops. I was happy because soon fifty per cent of all my business was on the Internet, but I was also keeping all my retail business at the same time.'

Then Geoff had a big stroke of luck. 'The amount of head shops sky-rocketed in 2012. Virtually all these new businesses had heard about my reputation and came to me for their supplies. Soon, the barn was filled to the brim with boxes of drugs but they were going out as fast as I could get them in. It was a dream scenario for any new business. After all those years of struggling I'd hit upon something that was fast turning me into a millionaire.'

However – and some would say inevitably – that was when the 'wrong sort of people' started taking an interest in Geoff's business. He explained: 'I guess it was kind of obvious it would happen but both the tax people and a bunch of local villains started looking rather closely at me. The tax people wanted to know how I was managing to shift so much of my "farm produce" so suddenly and I think they suspected I was involved in some kind of VAT fraud, which was not actually the case.

'I was outraged to be accused of such a thing. Then it dawned on me that they must have worked out I was selling legal-high products. An accountant friend of mine warned me that the tax people would want to try and prove I was living off criminal proceeds and couldn't deal with the fact I was just a normal, hard-working businessman who happened to have stumbled on a lucrative trade. It took me six months of audits including three "raids" by Revenue and Customs before they finally accepted that I was not breaking the law or trying to avoid tax.'

But no sooner had Geoff got the authorities off his back then he was faced with another much more sinister organization. He explained: 'I got a visit from a local drug baron. It was all very friendly at first. He turned up at my barn uninvited and asked about my prices and whether I'd be interested in selling him a large quantity of produce for a bargain price. I was a bit slow off the mark and laughed in his face when he offered me peanuts.

'Then in a split second the expression on his face completely changed. He stared right at me in a very chilling manner and just said: "I ain't offering. I'm tellin' you that's what I am gonna pay."'

Geoff went on: 'I was stunned. I'd been a bit naive at first but now I felt as if I was staring down the barrel of a loaded shotgun. I took a big gulp and told him that I didn't have enough produce in the barn at that time and I'd have to get it in first. He left with a big smile on his face after giving me his card and ordering me to call him as soon as the products were in.'

Geoff went on: 'I was panic-stricken. Here was this criminal who was threatening the very fabric of my business, which I had spent years building up. I didn't know what to do so I went and saw a local bobby whom I'd met a few times in the pub and who'd seemed a reasonable sort of fellow.

'I told him about this criminal and he promised to talk to his superiors and come back to me. Meanwhile, the drug baron started pressurizing me for the produce. I made up some excuse about the supplies being held up in China to buy myself some time.

'Meanwhile my friend the local bobby came back to me with some very bad news. He explained that not only were the police unwilling to help me but they warned me in no uncertain terms that they were "not happy" I was even running a legal-high business.

'It was a big blow because the police had effectively cut me loose and told me I had to face this villain all on my own. I found out later that this same drug baron actually had a "friend" in the local force and he'd tipped him off and they refused to do anything because the criminal threatening me was an informant for the local CID. I was stuffed on all fronts!'

Meanwhile the drug baron himself turned up back at Geoff's barn with a couple of 'associates' wanting to know about his produce. Geoff explained: 'Basically they threatened to burn the place to the ground if I didn't *give* them exactly what they wanted. There was no more talk of buying produce from me. They were simply attempting to take over my entire business for nothing. I was steaming angry inside but I knew it would be a mistake to get into an argument there and then, so I held my tongue and told them to give me a week to put my business in order before the hand-over. Just saying the word hand-over made me feel physically sick.'

Seven days later, the mobster and six more of his 'associates' turned up at the barn. 'I felt cornered,' Geoff recalled. 'I'd played the nice guy for long enough. Then twenty local gypsies who I'd hired to help me to hump crates and stuff in the past walked out from behind the barn armed with baseball bats and gave these villains a big scare. They sorted out the gangsters. It was hand-to-hand or rather fist-to-fist stuff but my guys had their baseball bats and they were prepared to use them. The gypsies crushed the criminals in minutes but it was not a pretty sight.

'I knew it was a big risk but a friend of mine had told me that if I didn't stand up to them and hit back very hard they'd probably walk all over me. This way they might actually leave me completely alone and he was proved totally right. The criminals retreated like hobbling hyenas never to be heard of again. I had taken one hell of a risk but it worked.'

From then on, Geoff's legal-high supply business went from strength to strength. 'It's booming today and the turnover goes up by at least thirty per cent each year. Just after my run-in with the villains I decided to buy a much larger warehouse on a local trading estate and go legit, so to speak. I've also managed to purchase a house nearby. My bank manager is so impressed he keeps offering me more loans that, quite frankly, I don't even need. It's been one hell of a journey but I don't regret a moment of it.'

In 2013, Geoff met and fell in love with a woman who owns a head shop close to his warehouse. 'Sometimes I can't quite believe that all this is down to legal highs. Five years ago my life was in tatters. I was heartbroken after my marriage broke down and I was virtually destitute. Now things are so good. All the pieces are falling together nicely and I hope that soon I'll maybe find a genuine buyer for the business rather than a bunch of crooks who thought they could bully me out of what was rightfully mine.'

Geoff wasn't the only man I met who found that making a success of the legal-high business meant he could rescue a life that had previously looked to be going down the pan.

CHAPTER 18

FRANK

Driving along in his high-powered sports car near Marbella, in southern Spain, Frank explained how he was making more money than the illegal drug dealers who swamp so much of this area. Frank claimed he'd tapped into a rich vein of customers – nearly all aged under thirty-five – who've turned their backs on cocaine and Ecstasy in favour of legal highs. Frank reckoned his business was relatively risk free but he admitted he was always on his guard in case rival criminals tried to 'take an interest in my business' which 'would end in a bloodbath'.

But then Frank knows all about bloodbaths and prison; back in the late 1990s, he got a lengthy sentence thanks to his membership of a notorious Spanish-based gang of British ex-pat coke smugglers. After doing his time, Frank came out determined to find a way to make big money without getting on the wrong side of the law.

'I've seen the nasty side of the drug business and it's deadly,' said Frank, now close to fifty and looking forward to one day soon retiring to his villa in the hills overlooking the Costa del Sol. 'The legal-highs trade has got this reputation for being full of young airheads so I suppose characters like me give legal highs a bad name. My background is in the real old-fashioned illegal drug trade but I'm fuckin' relieved I'm out of that game. It was a hairy time back here in the 1990s. The place was awash with cocaine and every Tom, Dick and Harry was trying to make a few bob out of smuggling it.

'Back then a couple of brothers were involved in the coke trade out here and they persuaded me to come over from the UK and give them a hand. It was the biggest mistake of my life. Back in London, I'd been an electrician by trade and my mum was mighty proud that I hadn't become a villain like my two brothers. I should have just kept to myself and plodded along in London. I had a wife and two kids, a council house and a calm, simple life.

'Then I flew out to Spain for my brother's stag party because he was getting married and that was the beginning of the end.' Frank admitted: 'I immediately fell for the coke, the wine, the women and the song all in one big hit.' He continued: 'I was such a fool. I never went back to London after that stag party. I met a beautiful Dutch girl and I thought it was love at first sight. What a fuckin' idiot I was!'

Initially, Frank tried to get work as an electrician within the English community of 250,000 who lived on the Costa del Sol at the time. 'I didn't even have the courage to go back to London and give my missus a chance for us to get back together. I dumped her and the kids in a phone call. I'm deeply ashamed of it all.

'But cocaine had taken a grip on my life by then. I'd never even touched the stuff before I got to my brother's stag party. My work as an electrician was barely paying the rent on my tiny apartment, let alone stretching to pay for drugs. The Dutch woman dumped me for a richer man, who turned out to be one of the wealthiest cocaine barons on the coast. I was out of my depth, mixing with horrible nasty villains who'd shoot people and ask questions later. It was like going onto the set of a real-life version of *Scarface*. I look back on it now as a living nightmare.'

Within months, Frank was working as a 'transporter' for a cocaine baron, who employed one of his brothers. 'My brother told me this guy was a lot nicer than most of them and that it would tide me over until I got my electrician work properly up and running. What a mug I was. This outfit had me driving shipments of coke up through Spain, into France and then across the channel to the UK. They paid me quite well but it wasn't worth it.

'The first time I did a run, I found myself sweating buckets and just waiting to be nicked at Customs in Dover. It was horrible and I literally threw up with nerves. Then I took the opportunity to go and see my ex-wife and kids since I was back in London for the first time since I'd abandoned them all. Well, it was a stupid move on my part. My wife was so upset I'd turned up at their house that she called the police and then told them I was a criminal in front of them. I didn't realize that one of my oldest friends had told her all about my new career as a drugs transporter.

'That incident helped the police mark me down as a suspicious character because on the next run back from Spain I was nicked. There was £500,000 worth of coke hidden in a gas tank and I was hauled off to court.'

Frank did five years after the judge took pity on him because it was clear he was not the man behind the drug gang. 'I suppose I was lucky cos he could have sentenced me to at least ten years on account of the amount of coke I was carrying. But I was gutted. In the space of a year, I'd lost my family, my job and my liberty. I had nothing but the clothes I stood in.'

But things then took an even worse turn, as Frank went on to explain. 'The boss of the gang I was working for felt sorry for me and promised to look after my family while I was inside. But my ex went ballistic when some bloke turned up at the house with an envelope of cash and she called the police again. This made the bossman go crazy and I never spoke to him or his people ever again. So now I'd been completely cut loose and it felt very lonely.'

Unlike most prisoners who spend their sentences planning new crimes to commit as soon as they're released, Frank studied hard to improve his knowledge and even ended up taking a university degree while in jail. 'I'd always been interested in chemistry and stuff like that so I took a degree on that subject and that's how I stumbled on legal highs.

'They'd just started hitting the Internet and I spotted that there was no quality control whatsoever. When I'd been involved in the coke game, I'd noticed that there were strict quality controls, even though the stuff was highly illegal. But that was down to paranoid drug barons wanting to make sure they were not sold fake product. The safety of the punters was not high on their list of priorities. But I realized that my experience in the coke trade might actually help me in relation to legal highs.'

Frank claims he studied hard and achieved a 2:1 chemistry degree inside prison. 'That specialist knowledge helped me realize how simple it was to create some of these legal highs yourself. The formulas were often very simple, but most important of all, it wasn't illegal to produce them.

'I kept wondering what the catch was. How could it be so simple? I even thought the fact they were called legal highs might work against them in a sense. In other words, people would not be so attracted to them because there was no risk involved in taking them. I soon realized the key to the business was to come up with products that virtually mirrored illegal substances like cocaine and cannabis.'

Within weeks of being released from prison, Frank discreetly purchased a wide range of legal highs and began testing the products to see precisely what ingredients were in them. 'I soon discovered it was a lottery and in many ways a lot more potentially dangerous to the customers than the illegal stuff. These naive kids were buying what they thought were legal and safe drugs while in fact the opposite was true. I thought about all my experiences within the illegal drug trade and realized I needed to set up supply chains and routes for legal highs.

'There are literally millions of potential customers just sitting there waiting to buy legal highs yet the business itself was surrounded in secrecy and to be honest about it, it felt as criminal as dealing in coke.'

He explained: 'The comparisons with the coke game don't end there, either. Legal highs even follow a similar route when they're brought into the UK. I remember when I was smuggling coke most of it went through the hub of Rotterdam in Holland. Well, guess what? That's where a lot of the legal-high stuff comes via, too.

'More and more legal highs are being knocked out in factories in the old Eastern Bloc countries. They're desperate for business and undercutting virtually all the legal-high producers in China and India. Trouble is that a lot of the Eastern European product is rubbish. It's not even worth the transport charges. They're always takin' the piss over there. They think that no one will notice that a legal high sold as a coke-type drug is nothing more than chalk dust or dried baby milk. It's a stupid short-term attitude as you can't make big money out of this game without repeat customers. It was the same with coke.

'If the stuff doesn't hit the spot then people move on to other suppliers. It's as simple as that. When I first started dealing with the Eastern Europeans I decided I needed to take a look at their factories. Well, it was like going into the cocaine badlands. The characters were just as dodgy as those in the coke and hash business and it was crystal clear to me these people were in it for a quick hit of cash. They didn't understand the importance of a quality product.'

But Frank didn't give up on Eastern Europe. 'I wanted to find someone who was honest enough and clever enough to let me decide on the contents of each product and then I'd let them produce it for me in high numbers. It took four months of travelling back and forth to Romania and Albania before I found a guy who actually got it.

'His name was Christov and he and I got on like a house on fire. He also happened to be the first legal-high producer in Albania who wasn't armed when I met him! This guy was as hard as nails but he understood the need for quality over quantity. I invested a lot of time in him and we began producing our own version of a brilliant Ecstasy-type legal high called PMA, which I knew would sell well on the party and club scene throughout Europe, especially in Spain and the UK.

'Soon we were mass-producing 50,000 tablets a week at Christov's factory in Albania. That would then be exported to Rotterdam where it was then dispersed to various countries where I'd set up supply chains. Sounds just like cocaine smuggling, eh? In fact, after the first few shipments I got pulled by the law in Spain. They were convinced I was smuggling illegal drugs, until I invited them along to my warehouse near Malaga and showed them the produce. At that time PMA and all its derivatives were legal.

'They still thought I was an old-fashioned E dealer so I gave them samples and told them to go away and test them. They came back two weeks later laughing and telling me that I was completely in the clear. The great thing about the Spanish police, probably compared to most countries, is that they understand the need for young people to experiment and they see legal highs as something a lot more healthy than illicit drugs.'

Frank believes that many street dealers pass off PMA as real Ecstasy but he insisted that was not his problem. 'Listen, I know it's a lot like E and that's why it eventually got banned but my version wasn't quite the same as what others call PMA.'

In Spain, Frank says he was treated like an ordinary businessman. 'The chief of police here even invited me to attend a local police conference on drugs during which I was offered lab facilities to test all my products to make sure the ingredients were safe as well as legal.

'This was an extraordinary development because it meant the police were in effect sanctioning my products and I could honestly say they had official approval. I even used that to help convince some of my bigger customers about the safety aspects of many of my legal highs and that made them even more appealing to a wider range of customers.'

But over the past two years, Frank claims the legal-high business has 'got much trickier'. He explained: 'That PMA type stuff I was flogging like hotcakes got outlawed and in the end I had to use completely different ingredients and, quite frankly, it didn't sell as well. I guess that was kind of inevitable.

'I've also noticed that quite a few villains are looking at starting up legal-high businesses because their coke and cannabis is so impure that a lot of people are beginning to look for alternatives. I've heard that the American mafia are even trying to get a toehold in the legal-high business because they believe it's going to make them a fortune in the near future.

'That's the last thing I want. I got into this business to get away from trigger-happy villains. Also, if the heavier sort of criminals try to take over the legal-high business then it will force the authorities in many countries to stamp down even harder on the business.

'The main reason why I operate out of Spain is because they are slower at outlawing many substances. In the UK and other parts of Europe laws are being passed all the time to outlaw certain legal highs. But all this does is force the suppliers to simply tweak a product sufficiently so it doesn't come under that specific legal ban. It also plays into the hands of the heavy drug gangs who can then push the product around at inflated prices.'

Frank claimed that at least one gang of American gangsters has been pouring money into a number of factory sites in Eastern Europe in order to flood the US with legal-high products. 'That's what I heard. They're trying to keep it low-key but if I know about it then you can be sure that many others do too. Those Americans need to tread carefully because you have to bribe a lot of people in Eastern Europe. Old-time villains don't really appreciate just how deadly the Eastern Europeans can be. A lot of these characters are a law unto themselves in their own countries.'

Frank said he knew of one gang of French criminals who started up two factories in northern Romania 'and it really kicked off. The French bunged a few bob here and there and believed that gave them the right to control everything at these factories. Then they went and fell out with the local guys, who were running the factories for them. The French boys were so angry at being ripped off that they went to Romania and demanded their money back.

'Boy, did they get a shock when they turned up on the doorstep of one of the locals, who'd been running things for them. The Romanians were armed with automatics and machine guns. I heard that only three of the French gangsters got out alive and they were only spared because the Romanians wanted them to spread the word in France to make sure no one else ever came back.'

Frank said he continued to use 'a bit of bribery and corruption' to ensure his products were safely transported. 'It's outrageous really but I have to grease a lot of palms both here in southern Spain and in Albania to ensure all my products reach their customers on time. It was so bad to start with, I used to insist all the products came to me here in Spain first and then I would distribute them but that ended up causing me a lot of headaches with the Customs people here, so I decided to try and get it all dispersed direct from the factory in Albania.

'It's been a bloody nightmare because the Albanians expect bribes for letting anything across their borders, whether it is legal or not. I've now managed to get a representative over there who gets the stuff through for me but it still takes ten per cent of my profit off the top of each order.'

Frank added: 'My next targets are Ukraine and Russia. The legal-high markets in those places are relatively untapped. Sure, I know they have a few problems in Ukraine at the moment but I always consider one important factor when it comes to finding lucrative new legal places to start selling to. If cocaine has flourished in the past then legal highs will be sure to follow and that is definitely the case with Kiev and Moscow. They are currently awash with coke from what I've heard.'

Frank's Spanish-based legal-high business continues to thrive. He says: 'Now for the first time I can relax and take my foot off the pedal, safe in the knowledge that I'm not breaking any laws here and, for the moment, the underworld is leaving me in peace. I just hope it continues this way.'

Meanwhile, the comparatively new phenomenon of legal-high dealers thrives in one of the world's most famous cities.

CHAPTER 19

DENNY

Denny is an Irish-born 'entrepreneur' based in New York, who claims to run a successful legal-high home delivery service. Denny says his drugs are available 'any time of the day or night' and offers a service to customers that is akin to ordering a takeaway pizza.

I met Denny in one of NYC's numerous Irish bars. Dressed in a tie, a crisp blue shirt and a lightweight suit, he looked more like a city trader than a supplier of exotic legal highs.

'I like being smart because that surprises people. Why should I wear jeans and look like a hippy just because I deal in drugs? This is my way of telling people that I'm a serious dude and this is my full-time job.'

Denny admitted he had little idea what was in the legal highs he supplied, except to say: 'I guarantee they work! Legal highs are big news here in the States. They're considered a safe alternative to stuff like heroin and coke. The cops are constantly trying to get all legal highs banned and even the revenue [tax] people are now getting in on the act. If the police don't get you then the taxmen raid your bank account and steal all your money and claim it has come from dishonest earnings. Luckily I keep all my money somewhere much safer than a bank.'

So how and why did Denny get into the legal-high business in the first place? 'I had a decent regular job here in NYC for the first couple of years after I came out from Ireland. But the pay was crap and I was living in a filthy hole of an apartment across the river. It got so tough I seriously thought about going home to Ireland. New York can be a cruel place to be if you're broke and without friends.

'But then I got in with this crowd of guys – a lot of them were also Irish – and we started taking legal highs, which we mostly got off the Internet. It was a bit of a joke at first because about seven out of ten of everything we bought was useless! I started to realize that the Internet was actually destroying the legal-high business in a sense because people were being ripped off all the time since you were buying the stuff from faceless people hiding behind websites.

'It took me a few months partying with this crowd of guys to work out which of the legal highs really worked. Then I started reading the Internet chatrooms and stuff like that and realized there was this whole subculture of people taking legal highs, who were suffering from exactly the same problem: lack of quality produce. Some people were even saying they'd gone back to hash and coke because they were so sick of being ripped off by legal-high websites.

'The trouble was that buying legal highs online wasn't like buying a shirt and finding it was too small and then sending it back. You can't do that once you've opened the packet and taken some! It was giving the whole legal-high business a bad vibe, especially in the States where people are far more proactive if they think they're being ripped off. There is this corporate mentality even when it comes to drugs!

'Anyway, all this got me thinking about whether I should start a business supplying good-quality legal highs, which I'd deliver direct to customers. I knew from previous experience that New Yorkers usually go out on the street to buy their drugs from dealers but these narcotics were legal so surely I could deliver them to their homes?

'I bounced the idea around a few people and it got a very good response. I started out very small by simply offering my service to people I met in bars and clubs when I was out with my friends. But I was soon getting daily calls and it was clear I had tapped into something big. I began to realize New Yorkers were the perfect legal-high customers because they aren't risk takers and I was enabling them to take drugs without any of the usual hassle.

'One time I met this real drug dealer who worked on Times Square and pushed cocaine. He was a very funny guy and he told me that he usually sold crushed-up mints and pretended it was cocaine. That sort of summed up the situation perfectly because at least my products were real!'

Denny – who opened his business in 2012 – claimed he had a hardcore of about 300 customers who bought legal highs from him every week. 'But sometimes they put in really big orders if they're having a party or something like that. On a couple of occasions, I've even been paid to travel upstate with dozens of tablets and sachets for groups of people staying in cabins and stuff like that.'

Denny recalled that he once received an order for 1,500 packets of tablets and powder from a well-known actor staying in a rented house on the beach in the so-called millionaire's seaside resort of Southampton, north of New York City. 'That was really wild. I went up there and ended up staying as this guy's guest for the whole weekend. It was crazy because a lot of the people who came round each night were completely straight and would have been horrified if they'd known this actor and his closest friends were on legal highs pretty much all the time.

'I asked this actor why he liked to have so many legal highs in one stash and he told me he was about to go to Morocco and Europe to make a big budget movie and that as it would be so boring he was planning to take the stuff with him and give it to his friends on the movie set. He was a good guy and I was delighted when he got in touch a year later when he came back to New York. He's remained one of my best customers ever since.'

Happy-go-lucky Denny claimed he hadn't had one bad

experience during his career. 'I think that sorta sums it up, doesn't it? The people I buy from are just names on an email, not vicious criminals out to kill anyone who upsets them. The customers I deal with are usually gentle, fun-loving people who don't want to break the law. It couldn't be more different from dealing illegal narcotics.

'I'm extremely happy in my job too. And let's face it, there can't be many old-fashioned illegal drug dealers who could say that, are there?'

But there remain many aspects of the legal-high trade that resemble the illicit drug business. Denny explained: 'I don't give people my real name and I never allow anyone to come to my place to score. Those are my two golden rules and I'm glad I've stuck with them because you can never be too sure what lies around the corner, can you?'

What about Denny's future in the legal-high trade? 'I have no plans to quit,' he replied, 'but I can tell you I'll know when it's time to get out of this business. I am convinced that many of my customers actually like the balance between taking a legal substance but still having a dealer come to their house. There is this strange vicarious thrill people seem to get when you turn up with a choice of drugs to offer them. They're all so excited that you're there.'

Denny's job may take him into the homes of some of America's rich and famous but back in the UK, the legal-high trade often finds itself in far humbler circumstances.

CHAPTER 20

TRACEY, HEATHER, KELLY AND LINDA

Four young single mothers found themselves looking at life's scrapheap until they discovered how to make 'bundles' of cash from the legal-high trade. Tracey, Heather, Kelly and Linda set up shop on the council estate where they live fifty miles north of London. They say they're not proud of what they've done but their drugs co-operative is not unique by any means.

'Three of us went to school together and when we found ourselves on the dole with kids and no one to support us, we started looking round for ways to make some extra cash,' recalled Heather. 'We all go clubbing now and again and legal highs were around but we kept noticing that you couldn't get them easily enough and most people don't think about getting them until they are often halfway through a drunken evening.'

Her friend Linda went on: 'It's dead easy to get hold of them and as far as we're concerned we're not doing nothin' wrong cos they're legal, aren't they?'

The four women proudly insisted they'd even managed to avoid problems with local gangsters who sell speed and coke in their neighbourhood, as Kelly explained: 'They're still banging out all the old-fashioned stuff. They seem to turn their noses up at what we do. They actually think they're above selling legal highs. Long may it continue because we're exploited that market brilliantly.'

The four women take it in turns each week to use their flats as a base to sell from. 'It's a good system because it means we can control who comes knocking,' explained Linda. 'And that we also avoid nosy neighbours, who would just presume we were normal drug dealers and call the police.'

The four women even change mobiles every month to avoid any difficulties. 'You have to be on the careful side, otherwise something bad could happen. We like to think that while we might appear to be four young mums trying to make a few bob, we are actually very professional in the way we run this business.'

The four women are fond of emphasizing the word 'legal' in their 'legal highs' business, but privately they admitted many of the substances they sell are 'at the very least border-line illegal'. Kelly explained: 'We know a lot of this stuff is outlawed soon after it comes on the market, so we try not to discuss that side of things with anyone. We have about fifty hardcore customers, most of whom come to us at least once a week. It's certainly true that a lot of them could easily order the same stuff off the Internet but most people round these parts don't have bank accounts or credit cards and they prefer to deal in cash and that's where we come in.'

Kelly said it was highly likely that she and her three friends were 'most probably on a police watchlist' but, for the moment, the local force had not bothered them. 'There is a lot of crime round these parts so they haven't got time to start hassling us,' she said. 'We make sure we don't rub people's noses in it, either.'

Linda explained that all four women knew full well that one day their business would have to be closed down. 'Let's face it, we're not going to be flogging this stuff in five years' time, are we?' she asserted. 'It will all have been outlawed by then and hopefully, we'll have moved on with our lives.'

Only recently, the police in their area had broken up a mephedrone gang following a two-year investigation. It eventually led to the arrest of fifteen offenders over a six-month period, during which more than fifty bags of mephedrone were recovered. But the four women insisted they did not deal in that particular substance. 'It's evil stuff and we don't touch it. That gang selling it were bloody idiots because it's lethal and the police treat it as bad as dealing in coke and heroin, which was why they all got banged up for flogging it.'

One of the detectives who arrested the gang of Meow Meow dealers said at the time: 'Some of the defendants recognize the harm that "meph" causes and the damage it has done to their own lives and health as a result. Those defendants have been sentenced sympathetically. Other defendants have shown complete and utter contempt of the consequences and effects of their criminal activity, even to the point of continuing to supply the drug to children despite it causing the individual themselves to be seriously ill.'

Heather explained why they were different from that gang: 'Look, our kids are the main priority in our lives. We don't want to lose them so we tread very carefully. Those idiots selling Meow Meow got what they deserved. They were shouting it from the rooftops and they didn't seem to give a toss what happened to the kids they were supplying. Having children ourselves makes us think twice about the whole issue of health because obviously none of us would want our kids to die of an overdose.'

CHAPTER 21

TREVOR

In the UK and numerous other European countries it's reckoned that many clubbers are polydrug users – in other words they regularly take legal highs alongside Ecstasy and cocaine. Experts warn that this is a trend that could pose profound risks to their health. Increasing numbers of legal-high consumers are suffering heart attacks and other serious illnesses, apparently brought on by a combination of legal highs and illegal drugs.

This mixing of different narcotics clearly implies that criminalizing drugs has had little effect on consumption, other than to provide new revenue streams for dealers selling established illicit substances.

So it's no big surprise that polydrug dealers like Trevor have emerged on the legal-high horizon. On the infamous party island of Ibiza – regarded by many as the clubbing capital of the world – he and other British criminals are dealing in legal highs alongside regular drugs such as cocaine and Ecstasy. They claim this decision has been driven mainly by a huge demand for *any* drugs from Britons visiting during the busy summer months on the Mediterranean island.

Trevor hails from Eastbourne, in East Sussex, but for the past three years he's moved over to Ibiza every summer. 'It's a dreamscape scenario for me,' said Trevor. 'I deal in a bit of coke that I buy locally but my main business these days is legal highs. I buy them all back in the UK and bring them over.'

Trevor said he had no fears about being busted by the local police. 'They're really cool. They see all this stuff in proper packaging and don't even consider it illegal in any sense. Mind you, I'm not sure they even understand the words "Not fit for human consumption"!'

He revealed that on arriving on Ibiza in the summer of 2013, he had his cases searched by suspicious police who opened one bag containing 'hundreds of legal highs'. Trevor went on: 'They took them all out of the bag and started studying them. Then the only one who spoke any English asked me if they were "sweets". I was about to tell him the truth when his friend winked at me and I realized they knew perfectly well what was in them but they were not prepared to nick me for them.

'A few moments later, they helped me repack my bags and I was off on my way to my villa. As far as I was concerned they were as good as encouraging me to sell legal highs. Obviously they were looking for cocaine and when I didn't have any they simply waved me on.'

Trevor claimed that Ibiza was 'cool about legal highs' long before he started working there in 2011. 'It's certainly true. I reckon their attitude is that they've got enough on their plate dealing with all the old-fashioned drugs, so the last thing they want to do is get bogged down with legal highs. One copper told me in a bar once that they don't believe legal highs are harmful, so they simply don't prioritize them.'

Trevor insisted he was not aware of any deaths or injuries connected to legal highs on his 'watch' in Ibiza. 'Of course some kids go way over the top but I can honestly say that no one has come to any harm after taking a product I sold them. Most of us are getting on with our business very low-key here. I actually feel sorry for the cops when they get the runaround from old-school villains, who swamp the island with coke and weed every summer. These cops just want an easy life and then some trigger-happy dude goes and sign-posts what he is doing by spraying his Uzi in all directions. It's out of order. I like to keep a low profile.'

Trevor is so laid back about his stays on Ibiza that he even takes his wife and young child with him when he rents a detached villa each summer. 'It's interesting because the sort of people who take legal highs tend to be much less abrasive than the lot who do coke. I don't even mind them coming to my house for a purchase because all I do is pull a packaged bag out of my case and give it to them, so what's the harm in that?'

Trevor admitted he made up to 300 per cent mark-up on

the legal highs he sold in Ibiza. 'I call that my "handling charge". The funny thing is that some legal highs are available in shops here but they tend to be the more hardcore, less tested substances, which a lot of people are very wary of buying. Also the packaging is in Spanish, so most Brits haven't a clue what they say, which makes people even more careful.'

Trevor went on: 'Not one customer has ever accused me of ripping them off. They accept my mark-up because it makes them feel much more secure to be taking a product that is covered in English words.'

Trevor claims that back in his UK base in London the legal-high business is much more tightly controlled and he doesn't sell the same volume of products on home turf. 'I make a lot of money out of those two or three months in Ibiza. It's a much heavier scene here in London so I keep that side of the business very small, although I still supply some lazy customers, many of whom are the same ones who decamp to Ibiza every summer.'

Now in his mid-thirties, Trevor said he was already planning a 'long and happy retirement' from the legal-high business. 'I'm on course to save up enough money to buy a second home in France, where my wife comes from. I reckon in another three or four years the legal-high market will be so flooded with dealers and products that there won't be enough business to go round. That's when I'll quit.'

Trevor said he never takes any drugs himself. 'Best way, I reckon. It means when the customers start complaining about the quality I simply tell them, "Sorry, I don't do them", so they can't get on my case about it.'

Trevor admitted the purity of the legal highs he supplied 'varied enormously'. He explained: 'As far as I'm concerned this is a business and I will do just about anything to ensure I make maximum profit. Sure, the stuff is quite random but it still has enough of something in it to work, otherwise I'd soon run out of customers.'

Trevor claimed one of his best clients in the UK and during the summer months on Ibiza is a well-known member of an iconic rock group. 'This guy is loaded. Some weeks he buys as much as 100 packets off me and last summer on Ibiza he put in orders for 50 grams of one product called Kokaine in just a week. I think he fobs all of it off on his friends and keeps some real coke aside for himself.'

If the attitude of the Spanish police is anything to go by then Trevor might well last a lot longer on Ibiza than on the streets of Eastbourne. Underpaid and understaffed, they are facing a round-the-clock struggle against the cocaine barons, so they are unlikely to bother with purveyors of legal narcotics.

PART FOUR

TESTERS/DEALERS/PRISONS/ CONSUMERS – UK, SOUTH AFRICA, SPAIN, SCANDINAVIA

Kids are sending around party invites with a link on where to buy your drugs. The Home Office and police find that extremely difficult to get our heads around and we are flat footed.

Association of UK Chief Police Officers
drugs spokesman Tim Hollis

CHAPTER 22

LUCY

UK-based Lucy calls herself 'the ultimate guinea pig'. She makes what she described as 'decent pocket money' testing out new legal highs at the rate of 'two or three' a month. She explained: 'I get £100 for each legal high I try and it's a very useful additional income for me.'

Lucy works as an assistant in a vet's surgery near her home in Sussex. She first started taking legal highs in her late teens when she was a regular on the festival circuit in south-east England. 'I knew all about Ecstasy but all my friends said it was often complete crap and there was something much more appealing about taking something that was at least deemed to be legal and brand new. It made it more exciting in a sense. The first time I took a legal high was when I was fifteen. I told my mum and she was cool with it because the stuff wasn't illegal. Now looking back on it we were both incredibly naive because most of this stuff is never properly tested and I didn't really have a clue about what I was actually taking.'

Lucy eventually went off to university in Leeds and encountered many more legal highs on the club scene in that northern city. 'The main reason students took legal highs back then was because they were so cheap. The trouble with them was that more often than not they did absolutely nothing for you. I got fed up of it and stopped taking them altogether until I completed uni and moved back to Sussex.'

Back home, Lucy noticed that new legal highs were being made available all the time on the Internet. 'I couldn't believe it at first. There were so many different brands and types. By this time in my home town a lot of people under the age of thirty were experimenting with legal highs and I noticed that some of them seemed much more powerful than the ones I'd taken when I was at uni.'

Lucy admitted she'd never been afraid of drugs. 'I still dabbled quite a bit probably partly because I was bored and unemployed at the time. I'm not one of those people scared to try something new. I've always had an adventurous spirit and I like experimenting. I even had one or two bad trips on some new legal-high products but I still liked trying them now and again.

'Then one of my old friends from uni got in touch to say he was starting a website supplying legal highs. He remembered that I'd always been up for trying new stuff and asked if I would be interested in testing some of them for him.

Well, I was struggling to find work at the time and I also realized that legal-high customers needed to hear from someone they could trust about the quality of the produce. So my friend with the legal-high website agreed to pay me £100 for each one I tested.

'Some people reading this will probably think I was mad to agree to do such a thing but I needed the money and my friend and I agreed that if we didn't like the look of anything we'd ditch it before I tried it out. To be frank about it, I sort of get off on the feeling that I am going on a voyage into the unknown. I know that sounds a bit crazy but it's what I like.'

Lucy admitted, though, that she hadn't told many of her friends about her 'other job'. She explained: 'I haven't told any of my family and I've only told a couple of friends because I know it sounds like I'm being a bit stupid to take so many risks although I don't look on it that way.'

Lucy tried to explain what she meant. 'This is a very tricky balancing act. On the one hand I want to make sure that the customers on my friend's website buy products that will actually give them a high. But at the same time I don't want them to end up completely out of control because that might put them in a dangerous environment, if you see what I mean.

'Recently I took a legal high that was packaged up as a cocaine equivalent. I've had real cocaine so I was intrigued to see if this stuff could match it. Well, it did more than that! I went totally hysterical and hyped up on it and had to take some sedatives to calm myself down. Luckily I had some friends with me at the time so I knew I would be safe. Now some people will think I am plain stupid and that incident was a warning sign to stop all this testing immediately. But I didn't look at it that way.

'My attitude was that I had had a "bad trip" and now I knew that was a product to avoid, so the testing system had worked exactly the way it should. I wasn't freaked out about it. I just felt that this was a product which needed to be kept off my friend's website.'

Lucy's other 'duty' as a tester is to write up the bad legal-high products on blogs and other personalized Internet sources. She explained: 'It's a spin-off from what I do but it actually means that when I test something which is bad I can make sure that no one uses it any more. That can't be a bad thing, can it?'

Lucy admitted that the pay from her day job at the veterinary clinic was so low that she would continue to test legal highs 'for at least another couple of years'. As she pointed out: 'Obviously I can't do this for ever. It's probably not very good for my health and I'm twenty-six now, but I enjoy the process a lot.'

CHAPTER 23

VIC

Legal highs are supposed to be thriving because many young people have turned their noses up at the more familiar illegal drugs such as cocaine, heroin and cannabis. But during my research into the legal-high scene in London I came across increasing evidence of a disturbing development within the so-called traditional narcotics underworld.

Cocaine dealers are deliberately buying up huge quantities of certain legal highs that come in white powdered form and then passing them off as 'real marching powder'. One such dealer is Vic. He buys mephedrone for £20 a gram and sells it on as cocaine for at least £70 a gram. He explained: 'My punters seem to love it but then that's not so surprising because in recent years cocaine has been stepped on so much that this stuff is far more potent than most of the coke you can buy in London today.'

Vic's background reads like a history of London crime

over the past forty-five years. He couldn't be more different from the 'youngsters' who're supposed to be driving what's being described as a legal-high revolution.

'I've done it all, mate. I robbed banks. I held up security vans. I've transported drugs for the Colombians and I've seen the wrong end of a shooter on more occasions than I care to remember. My father was a villain before me and two of my boys seem to be heading on the same path as well. I'm not proud of that but where I come from in the Old Kent Road, "villainry" rules.'

Vic now lives in a comfortable detached house south of the capital but he was brought up in the notorious badlands of south-east London. 'I was out robbing and thieving from the age of twelve. That's just the way it was back then. The only people I looked up to as a kid were the Great Train Robbers. Most of them come from my manor and they were heroes to all of us. They stuck two fingers up at the establishment and pulled off a genius piece of work.

'By the time I left school at fourteen, I'd already accepted that my future lay in crime. All around me were these legendary characters, who proved to me that crime did pay. Me and my mates never had much time for school. We'd already educated ourselves by being streetwise and that was what mattered most of all back then.'

For the following thirty years, Vic found himself immersed in the London underworld and twice ended up 'serving long stretches' in prison for major bank robberies. 'Being in jail was just part of the job for me. I took it on the chin and made sure I didn't squeal on any of my mates and in exchange my family was looked after while I was away. It was a simple system and it worked well.'

But when he was released after his second spell in prison, Vic found that the underworld had undergone an enormous change. He explained: 'Robberies were finished. The police had won that war thanks to CCTV and all the other stuff which made it virtually impossible to pull off a big heist any more. So I drifted into the drugs trade and started transporting for a couple of big firms on my manor. They were all run by fellows like me who used to be professional blaggers, but had switched to drugs because it was a lot safer and usually much more lucrative.

'At first it seemed like very easy money. I organized all the shipments from Spain up to the UK and we had a very good airtight system that seemed to work like clockwork. But operations like that never last very long and, surprise, surprise, one of my team got nabbed by the Old Bill and they turned him into an informant. Next thing I know I'm being hauled into the nick and interrogated. It was no laughing matter. The police seemed to have me bang to rights but it turned out they was more obsessed with nicking the really big names who were financing the operation.

'So I did a deal. That doesn't mean I squealed. I just agreed to step away from working for those two firms because they had plans to put one of their own in there and monitor it all until they had enough evidence to nick the big boys. I knew I was treading on thin ice but I also knew I faced a fifteen-year stretch in prison if they nicked me again. The way I looked at it I wasn't actually informing on the two firms. Just getting out at the right moment.

'Somehow I managed to quit without raising any eyebrows, which in this game is a bloody miracle. But that left me in a huge vacuum with no proper source of income. I didn't know what to do next. All I knew about was villainry. I certainly couldn't handle a straight job. I'd reached a sort of crossroads where I had to make a big decision on which way to turn.

'I knew if I went back into the traditional drugs business then I'd soon be nicked and they'd make sure I was put away for a very long time. So I started looking around for something new and not so risky. One of my nephews owned a couple of clubs in East London and he gave me a bit of work as a doorman to tide me over. But it wasn't the sort of work I wanted for the long term.

'Now, I have occasionally dabbled in taking a bit of coke myself. I've seen a lot of people get completely fucked up by it but, taken in moderation, it's always seemed all right to me. One night I was out with a couple of mates and we bumped into an old boy who used to be a very big name in the robbery game. He slipped us a sachet of what we thought was coke and we popped off to the toilet and took a snort each.

'Well, it seemed a bit funny so when I went back to the table I asked this old boy where he got it and that's when he winked at me and said that it was something called Meow

Meow. I'd never heard of the stuff at that time, so it meant fuck all to me. But we got talking and he said he reckoned it was just as good as the white stuff. I wasn't so sure, but I could see the potential in it, especially since it was just another legal high back then. It hadn't even been banned. Now that's what got my attention. Here was this old boy handing out a secretive sachet of some old white shit and it wasn't even nickable.

'That got me thinking further. It looked like coke, vaguely tasted like it and more or less gave you the same high, sort of. And when he told me it cost 10 to 15 quid a gram, that was enough for me! In any case, the coke that was around by that time was only about five per cent pure, so this stuff seemed like a winner to me.

'Then I got an introduction to this Chinese bloke in Suffolk and bought ten grand's worth from him and got to work, selling it on to street dealers with a £25 mark-up per gram. Well, it sold like bloody hotcakes and no one complained about it. I reckon that's cos most people these days don't even know what a real line of cocaine feels like any more. It's cut to shit to keep the profits high. But with this stuff I didn't even need to bother cutting it with anything. In a sense it was as pure as driven snow, if you know what I mean.'

Then, ironically, Meow Meow was outlawed by the UK in 2010 as a dangerous substance and given a B classification. But that didn't put Vic off. 'I laughed when I heard they'd made it illegal because that was the very thing I was trying to avoid. I thought I'd have to stop flogging it but then my supplier announced that there was a simple solution: a new version under a different name. Well, that suited me fine because I'd been passing it off as coke, so what it was called on the open market made no difference to me. The main thing was that it had been played with so it wasn't strictly speaking Meow Meow and wasn't illegal.'

Today Vic reckons he has sold at least fifty different versions of Meow Meow as cocaine and not one of his customers has made a complaint. 'It's unbelievable when you think about it, but they all seem to trust me. I'm not even sure they care what it is as long as they can call it cocaine.'

Vic believes that the reason he's managed to pass off these substances as cocaine, is that none of his customers has ever actually had a snort of 'pure cocaine'. He explained: 'They just don't know what the real stuff tastes and looks like. Listen, I've seen so-called cocaine sold by dealers in London that is yellow and lumpy. The same dealers have turned up a week later with another batch that is white and powdery. But no one ever questions the quality or the look of it.

'Okay, these days it's considered a nickable offence to be carrying a large amount of any version of Meow Meow at any one time. But the price is still very low, so I just keep on banging it out.'

Vic sees the future in very simple terms. 'I've got no doubt that a lot more dangerous characters than me are after a piece of this type of action, so I'll probably walk away from it sooner rather than later. I heard on the grapevine that the

Eastern Europeans are setting up their own factories churning out the stuff and it's only a matter of time before they start flogging it in all our big cities. I've had dealings with those sort of foreign villains in southern Spain and I can tell you they're a bunch of fuckin' psychos. Once they get involved in the legal-high business there'll be guns going off in all directions.

'If I can just hold out for another year or so, I'll have enough cash to retire. It's a bloody miracle I've got to this age after some of the dodgy things I've been involved in. The key in this game is not to push your luck and get out while the going is good.'

CHAPTER 24

JETTY

There is the over-riding impression given throughout the world that legal highs are mostly the domain of the white middle classes. Jetty, based in Cape Town, is proud of his job as a legal-high dealer, even though he regularly clashes with the police and criminals, who consider him to be 'just another drug dealer' in their eyes.

Jetty explained: 'It's just the way it is out here. Everyone's desperate to earn some money and they get jealous if they see someone like me earning a lot of cash from something they don't even understand.'

Jetty recently had to turn for help to the father of one of his middle-class customers, who was a chief of police. 'I was being hassled by uniformed cops every day. I had to go into the gated communities where many of my best customers live and I was being stopped and searched and treated like an illegal drug dealer. I was sick of it, so I asked this guy's dad if he could help. It's not as if I was doing anything illegal because virtually no legal highs have been banned here in South Africa.

'Anyway, this guy's dad spoke to some of the officers and I was left in peace. It was a relief because I know they were wanting me to pay them a bribe because they are so lowly paid in this country. All normal drug dealers have to pay bribes to police as a form of tax. It comes with the job.'

Jetty believes his business thrives in South Africa because of the authorities' slowness in passing any legislation to ban the more dangerous legal highs. 'I know that in places like the UK and much of Europe a lot of legal highs have been banned by law, often very unfairly. But here everything I do is legal.'

Jetty reckoned business was booming because many of his mainly young customers use him to filter out the poor quality and often dangerous legal highs. 'I guess that's where I come in. These kids have tried to buy through the Internet but they don't know what to order and often end up with useless products which do not do what they're supposed to.'

Jetty got into the trade when he was dating the daughter of a local business tycoon. 'I was this kid from the wrong side of the tracks but I met this girl from a rich family. Then she introduced me to her very wealthy set of friends. One night a whole crew of us went out and took some legal highs on a nearby beach.

'Most of the stuff did nothing for us but a couple of people with us had some very scary experiences with something that turned out to be a legal-high equivalent to LSD. Anyhow, we got talking and they all said they'd much rather buy through someone like me so I decided to start my own legal-high business.'

Jetty talked in glowing terms about the different types of legal highs and how he could supply them all, for a price. His back-story provided a fascinating insight into the so-called 'acceptable face of legal-high dealing' and how it is offering some people a unique opportunity to escape the poverty trap in countries such as South Africa.

'I had nothing,' he recollected. 'No job. No prospects. No qualifications and I lived in a township with my mum. But I always wanted to do better. I was always on the lookout for an opportunity and that's why I went out with that rich girl and how I fell into this business. I don't tell any older people what I do for a living because they just wouldn't get it.

'I guess it's ironic that I run all the same risks as a regular drug dealer here. I get hassled by street gangsters who think I'm selling drugs on their territory. They know next to nothing about legal highs and just look at me as if I am mad whenever I try to explain what legal highs are.'

Jetty claimed that local criminals were so inquisitive about what he was doing that one gang followed him around for more than a month to try and get a handle on his business. 'It was outrageous. They didn't even bother hiding it from me. I think it was an attempt to intimidate me but it didn't work because I made sure I lost them each morning before I went to visit my first customer of the day. But it shows how confused the local criminals are by legal highs. Mind you, they might well one day try to intimidate my customers as well as scare me in order to take over my business.'

Jetty added: 'I don't know how long I will last in this business but I take each day as it comes. Average life expectancy for illegal drug dealers out here is about twenty-seven years old. I'm twenty-three and I want to live a long and happy life. I just hope all the bad people around me can let me live in peace.'

CHAPTER 25

ANNA

Based in a quiet mountainside *pueblo* overlooking the Spanish city of Murcia, in southern Spain, svelte Swedish-born Anna is an unlikely character to find in such an innovative, risky business. In her mid-forties with three teenage children, she owns and runs one of Spain's most successful legal-high websites and claims to be turning over upwards of 5,000 euros a week sending out packets of legal highs to customers all over Europe.

Behind her perfect teeth and plastic smile lies a steely determination to make a fortune out of legal highs. Anna reckons she has personally dispatched tens of thousands of packets of legal highs since setting up her business three years ago after her husband ran out on her, leaving her penniless.

'I'm in this for the money,' Anna said. 'There is no other reason. I would have lost my home and everything if I hadn't moved very quickly to find a business that could support me and my family after my husband left me. I've always closely monitored the Internet and I knew there was money to be made out of legal highs. But the key to being successful was to be based in a country that had a more relaxed attitude towards them.

'We were already here in Spain because my husband had been working as a property developer, so I started setting up my legal-high business very quickly. I knew the Spanish had a more laid-back attitude towards legal highs and I live a long way from any big cities so that meant I could run my business without flagging up my activities. My teenage son helped me set up my very first legal-high website but he understood from the outset that I did not want him or his brother and sister to start taking them under any circumstances.'

Anna operated her entire business from the garage of her house, which doubled as an office and warehouse for numerous boxes of legal highs that were stacked up to the ceiling. 'This is it. This is the operations room. It's pretty unimpressive, isn't it?' said Anna. 'But the beauty of this business is that I don't have to meet any of the customers face to face. I could be operating out of a tin shack on top of a mountain for all they know.'

Anna's prime marketplace for her products is Scandinavia. 'Obviously I speak the languages and I understand the way that Scandinavians think. I noticed there were very few companies like mine operating specifically for the

Scandinavian legal-high market. It's true that those countries have always been quick to ban certain legal highs but
that didn't mean there was no demand. For a while, however, it did create a climate of fear among many young
people in those countries. Also, it meant that any websites
actually based in Scandinavia could be closed down by the
authorities at any moment.'

Anna admitted her main website has been threatened
with closure by the Swedish authorities, who've accused her
of selling banned substances, but she claimed they gave up
pursuing her when they found out she was based in Spain.
'That was a good moment because it proved I was completely right to open my business here instead of in Sweden.
They are probably still monitoring my sites but they can't
do anything to stop me.

'So because I'm operating from Spain I was able to quickly
get a big slice of the market. I know from my own childhood
experiences just how bored most kids in Sweden and
throughout the rest of Scandinavia are. They're crying out
for legal highs especially since the governments of those
countries have been pretty good at keeping illegal drugs out
of their countries in the past.

'It's mad, isn't it? They cut off the suppliers of the illegal
drugs but now legal highs are available. There is a huge demand for them and part of the reason is that Scandinavians
missed out on drugs like coke and heroin. So legal highs
seem a bit naughty to the kids in those countries, many of

whom never went through the drug phase like in so many other countries.'

Spain is going through its worse depression since the thirties. But Anna believes she has managed to turn this to her advantage. She explained: 'Only a few miles down the road from here are dozens and dozens of empty warehouses built during the boom years but never occupied. I know I can rent them for next to nothing and I'm seriously thinking about setting up a lab down there and hiring in a couple of scientists to develop new legal-high products.

'I went to the local council recently to enquire if they would have any objection to me running such a business from there and they almost bit my hand off they were so desperate for anyone to set up a company. I actually think I could probably easily get a grant to cover the start-up costs.'

Anna says that in 2013, a notorious Spanish gangster approached her with a view to buying her business from her. She explained: 'I don't know any criminals but this guy had somehow heard all about my business and one day he just turned up here with a couple of henchmen and asked if he could have a chat with me. He was charming so it was difficult not to let him in.

'He then explained very calmly and politely that he'd been following my success and would I be interested in selling my company to him. I was astounded but I kept very cool and thanked him for his interest but then turned him down before he'd even had a chance to tell me what he wanted to pay.

'It was only a few days later it dawned on me that he probably wanted to use my site to sell legal highs and illegal drugs online. I guess I've built up the perfect template for such an operation. But that would be impossible for him to get away with and, in any case, my customers want legal highs not illegal drugs. Then a friend of mine pointed out that it was probably the boxes of legal highs he wanted in order to smuggle drugs in the same containers.'

Whatever the motivation of the criminal who approached Anna, she never heard from him again. She shrugged her shoulders and added: 'I'm sure others will approach me as my business continues to grow and I believe that one day I will have reached a point where it will be worth selling on the company but for the moment I want to keep expanding it.'

She added: 'I don't see that I have anything to be ashamed about. I make a living from legal highs. End of story.'

CHAPTER 26

MARK

The intention of most legal highs is to send people into a drug-induced haze. But there is a little known spin-off worth highlighting; using certain legal substances for weight loss has helped create a lucrative extra market for these designer drugs.

Mark, from Suffolk, had been struggling with his weight since his early teens but when he was sixteen he began using legal highs as appetite suppressants and he insists they worked. He explained: 'I had absolutely no interest in taking drugs of any type. I was always the odd one out at school because I didn't even take a drag on other people's cigarettes. The whole idea of risking my life by smoking, snorting or injecting something "foreign" into my body totally repulsed me.'

But all that changed the night Mark went out with a group of friends and one of them spiked his drink with a legal high known as BZP. He went on: 'I had absolutely no idea they'd done it. Looking back on it, it was a horribly irresponsible thing to do to a friend but what happened after I took it was very bizarre. I remember us all sitting round a table in a noisy pub and I kept noticing they were all watching me closely. Obviously I was the only one who didn't know their dirty little secret.

'Anyway, after about half an hour I started to feel very woozy and apparently – I can't remember much about that night – I asked to lie down on the bench alongside one of the tables in that pub. Then, instead of getting into some kind of drug groove, I simply went to sleep for two hours while all my mates danced the night away off their heads on various substances.

'From what they later said to me, they all felt rather guilty about spiking my drink and eventually woke me up and admitted what they'd done. Naturally, I was a bit freaked out by it but they made sure I got home safely and even helped me up to my bedroom without alerting my parents to what we'd all been up to. Next morning I woke up feeling a bit strange but I passed it all off as a bad experience and thought nothing more of it.

'But it's what happened next that is so surprising. Normally I'd have a massive breakfast of eggs, bacon, toast and cereal to set myself up for the day. Well, my mum called me downstairs to say my food was ready and I completely ignored the plate sitting on the table waiting for me and skipped out the door for a run round the block instead. It all felt seriously weird. I knew I was behaving strangely but I was also extremely happy to have ignored that gut cruncher of a breakfast for the first time in my life.

'That night I met up with all my friends again having eaten nothing more than a couple of apples and a banana and I felt a lot better than usual. It had already dawned on me during the day that those legal highs they'd spiked my drink with were probably responsible because they'd made my mind relax much more than usual but at the same time they'd given me an early morning boost of energy. And most important of all, I felt happier inside myself not to have eaten my usual daily intake of 4,000-plus calories.

'That night we went out again and this time I asked my friend to let me have more of the same legal high they'd spiked my drink with. This time I was up and dancing around and burning off even more calories. Next morning it was the same story, I struggled to manage to eat a bit of fruit and some dry biscuits. It was as if something inside me was finding my usual fatty foods repulsive.

'Well, for the next five days I took BZP every day and by the end of that week I'd lost half a stone but more importantly, my stomach had shrunk so much that my appetite began to reduce significantly. It was fantastic.

'Obviously there was a downside in that I was overly peppy that week. So I made a conscious decision not to take any more BZP for a few days and see if I could go cold turkey and still lose some more weight. Well, it worked a treat. I had, so to speak, got in the groove. I'm not particularly proud that my weight problems have been solved by legal highs but I have to say it was a most enjoyable way to lose weight because I was off my head much of the time!

'I've seen my own friends having huge problems while taking legal highs, so I don't want to sound like I'm advertising how wonderful they are. But in my case they sort of saved my life. I know that sounds twisted but it's the truth.'

However, three years later, Mark admitted he still occasionally uses legal highs. 'But now I actually take them for enjoyment purposes, although I like knowing in the back of my head that they're also helping me stay slim. My favourite product these days is something called "Beanz" which I found when I was at a festival in the West Country last year. It gives you what I think must be a bit of an amphetamine rush and I guess that must be what kills the appetite.

'Obviously I don't want to rely on legal highs for the rest of my life to keep slim but having my drink spiked all those years ago did me a huge favour. After all, I was on a downward spiral, my weight was ballooning. Back then I was so embarrassed I hardly ever went out and I'd become a virtual recluse like so many people with weight problems.

'Now I'm slim, healthy and a much happier person inside myself and I have a much more positive outlook on life.'

But there was an even more surprising coda to Mark's use of legal highs as an appetite suppressant. He explained: 'When I came out of college, I had plans to work in the media like so many kids these days. It was a nightmare trying to find a job. One TV company offered me a job for a year with no pay!

'Then one day I started googling and I found that the

same legal highs I took as a diet aid were still openly available on the Internet but no one had worked out they could be used as an appetite suppressant. They were still considered out and out party drugs.

'So I found the cheapest supplier of them and bought a big load of them. Then I created a website and started selling BMZ and Beanz as slimming aids. I even wrote my own personal experiences up as a way of recommending the products. I started social media sites to explain my previous weight problems and how those legal highs helped me conquer the calories.

'Well, you wouldn't believe how many hits I got within a week of putting that website online. It was incredible. So I decided to make the site even more blatantly just for people with weight problems. What a strange way to stumble on a well-paid career in the legal-high trade.'

Recently, Mark closed his website down after being 'visited' by health officials who wanted to know where he got his products from. 'That kind of scared me off. They traced me through my website and it felt a bit like Big Brother when they came knocking on my door asking awkward questions. They told me I wasn't strictly speaking breaking the law but that I needed to be extremely careful because new laws were about to be passed to stop rogue legal-high dealers from operating and I came under that category.

'So I pulled the plug on that slimmer's website although it had been a very interesting experience. I so enjoyed starting up my own business that I've now applied for a grant to start up a much more legitimate business.'

Prison inmates have always had surprisingly easy access to most illegal drugs inside jail but the surge in the use of legal highs in the 'outside world' has been mirrored behind bars, where they're just as easy to obtain.

Certain wings in UK men's prisons are said to be 'awash' with legal highs, despite attempts by authorities to crack down on smuggling all illicit materials into jails. It seems that prisoners prefer to smoke synthetic cannabis such as 'Spice' because it is currently not detectable in urine or blood tests.

Yet despite its undoubted presence inside Britain's jails, it seems that authorities have been extremely slow to crack down on inmates using legal highs. According to recently released former inmates at London's notorious Brixton Prison, legal highs are so common that they're used as 'currency' by inmates.

In July 2012, Brixton was 're-roled' down to a category C and D resettlement prison for the local area and as a result received a large influx of sex offenders. The prison was operating at about 60 per cent over its certified normal capacity at the time. Staff claimed they couldn't control the consumption of legal highs inside the prison because of the overcrowded conditions.

One ex-prison officer told me: 'Brixton is in a state of chaos. It's heavily overcrowded and when you work in a prison like that it's hard enough to keep the basics in check. You just haven't got the time to start turning cells over looking for things like legal highs. No wonder they've thrived.'

The same former officer also admitted: 'Staff don't like to admit it but often it's much easier to let inmates take drugs because you don't want confrontations with them. If I was working in a place like Brixton, I'd turn and look the other way when it came to legal highs. No doubt about it.'

In 2014, 30 per cent of prisoners told officials on a prison inspectors' visit to Brixton it was 'easy' and in some cases 'very easy' to get hold of legal highs. They even claimed it was three times easier than getting hold of alcohol or 'regular' drugs like hash and cocaine inside the prison.

But officials at HMP Blantyre, in Kent, blamed a spike in violence on the use of Spice. Inspectors claimed there had been a steep rise in incidents, including two serious assaults. They claimed the legal high – banned by law in 2009 – induced paranoia and had led to debt and bullying.

So who are the characters who've helped introduce legal highs to so many of Britain's male prisons?

CHAPTER 27

BRIAN

Brian was nicknamed 'Dr Feelbad' in the three prisons he served in during a five-year sentence for drug smuggling but he has provided a fascinating insight into the use of legal highs within the UK's penitentiary system.

'Legal highs are like a dream come true for people who're banged up,' Brian asserted. 'They provide inmates with an escape from the misery of prison and, to be honest about it, I managed to make enough cash from selling them inside that I had quite a few quid saved up when I got out.'

Brian is understandably worried that UK prison authorities might retrospectively prosecute him if they knew he'd been selling legal highs in prison, so he refused to reveal his real name. 'I gotta be careful. I don't even think most prison governors even know what legal highs are. This is something that's happening in a lot of prisons but no one appreciates it's going on most of the time. It's going to become a big problem soon because there are way more legal highs available than illegal stuff like coke and weed and they do pretty much the same thing.'

Brian claimed that despite being released from prison six months earlier, he'd set up a special legal-high supply route to certain prisons in the UK. He explained: 'I realized this was an untapped business when I was inside and I had the right connections so I've been supplying them through a couple of guys I know.'

Brian claims that orders are often made by prisoners with access to the Internet. 'You wouldn't believe how many inmates can use the net despite the regulations. We have special code words to make sure no one susses it out. The key to the business is that I can sell legal highs very cheaply compared with illegal drugs.'

Brian also claimed that numerous prison officers were prepared to smuggle legal highs into prisons. 'They seem to reckon they're pretty harmless compared with old-fashioned illegal drugs so they are more willing to smuggle them in. That's the beauty of calling them legal highs. Many of the screws reckon they'd get nothing more than a slap on the wrist if they were caught smuggling them inside.'

Brian revealed that some prison staff 'well below the level of governor' were unofficially encouraging the use of these synthetic narcotics. He explained: 'I've heard that legal highs are tolerated. It's a bit like allowing inmates TVs in their cells. It keeps them quiet and there are less unrest problems.

'One screw I know on the outside reckons legal highs are no different from prescribed tranquillizers. Sure, legal highs have been blamed for a couple of nasty incidents but I simply don't believe those stories. I think the authorities are just using that as a convenient excuse to clamp down on the inmates. It's typical.'

Brian makes a 300 per cent mark-up on all the produce he supplies to prisons but insists he is very careful only to supply popular brands. He explained: 'I have to watch my back for obvious reasons. Much of what I supply can be easily bought on the Internet or in a head shop.

'The brands are the most high profile because they're harder to trace back and most of them are packaged in a professional manner. This helps the screws if they're ever caught red-handed. They can say they didn't even see the harm in what they were doing and they can also be sure the packets have not been tampered with and contain illegal drugs.'

However, Brian says he's only in the business for the short term. 'I know the prison will come down hard on them in the end. The politicians will start kicking up a fuss and the next thing you know, taking legal highs will be a punishable offence.'

Brian conceded, however, that there were 'dosage problems' when it came to taking legal highs inside prison. He explained: 'A lot of inmates are so desperate for a "high" that they stuff back far too much in one go and that can cause severe health problems. In the prison where I completed my sentence, three inmates had to be taken to hospital in one evening just before I got out after overdosing on legal highs. In another prison I heard that two inmates actually died after taking legal highs.'

In both cases post-mortems found the inmates had taken substances that were considered 'legal' but were akin to the banned drug mephedrone. Another UK prison inmate died later the same month, according to Brian. He explained: 'That inmate had bought through one of my contacts. Sure, I felt bad about it but this guy took a massive overdose quite deliberately. I actually believe he did it to commit suicide but when they found out what was in his blood stream they blamed it all on legal highs.'

Brian said he'd heard from other inmates that the same man who died went into spasms and then blacked out completely before staff even bothered to try and help him. 'Apparently, his behaviour had become increasingly erratic. He'd been sold Super Spangle, Purple Bomb and White MM but he was told to be very careful not to take the whole lot as a cocktail. He should have just stuck to one at a time.'

Brian continued: 'D'you know what the stupid bastard did? He knocked back all three packets and then went completely AWOL and jumped out of a third-floor window. But nobody forced him to take those substances. He was an adult and he made the choice himself.'

These days, Brian says he is planning to turn over a new leaf and quit supplying legal highs and 'stick to the straight and narrow'. He explained: 'I used to kid myself into thinking that because they were called legal highs it was all right to flog them to anybody who wanted them, but those days are behind me now. I need to stick to straight work, otherwise I'll end up inside again. It's not a good business to be in when people are getting sick and sometimes even dying when they take them. I don't want that kind of responsibility on my shoulders.'

PART FIVE

THE UNITED KINGDOM OF LEGAL HIGHS?

Manufacturers turn these things around so quickly. One week you'll have a product with compound X, the next week it's compound Y. It's fascinating how fast it can occur, and it's fascinating to see the minute changes in chemical structure they'll come up with. It's similar, but it's different.

Forensic toxicologist Kevin Shanks of
AIT Laboratories, Indiana

The tiny Channel Island of Guernsey has evolved into something approaching a guinea-pig state for legal highs. For many years its strict anti-drugs policy prevented illegal drugs from ever flooding onto the island. But then legal highs came along and thanks to the Internet, a curious youth population who'd previously been deprived of old-fashioned drugs were suddenly given the keys to a narcotic playground.

The result is the world's highest usage of legal highs per head of population. Today other governments are watching developments in Guernsey closely. The island, which has a different legislative code to that of the UK, has struggled to balance its fear of encouraging the use of illegal drugs with the need to stay ahead of the flood of synthetic drugs by outlawing them as soon as they appear. At the moment it is a classic no-win situation.

One local detective summed up the dilemma: 'It doesn't matter whether drugs are legal or not, they cause the same social problems and we in Guernsey have unintentionally turned ourselves into a global guinea-pig nation when it comes to legal highs.'

LEGAL HIGHS

So how exactly did a tiny island become one of the world's most notorious legal-high states? My enquiries have uncovered that producers deliberately targeted the island from 2007 as the perfect test ground for their products. The use of legal highs remains prevalent on Guernsey, so I met with some of those users and suppliers to get a better insight into this unusual phenomenon.

CHAPTER 28

BOBBY, LENNY, CARLA AND JAMIE

My first port of call was a small, darkened warehouse on the outskirts of Guernsey's capital, St Peter Port. I met with Bobby, who claimed to be the island's most successful legal-high 'businessman'. Just a couple of miles down the road is this country's parliamentary building, where the politicians have been arguing about how to cope with this epidemic of legal highs that threatens the very fabric of this mainly conservative society. Bobby explained the ins and outs of the legal-high business and how the global recession affected his business. He disclosed the complexities of buying, distributing and selling large quantities of legal-high substances and where the future of the business was heading.

Bobby also claimed it was a ruthless business often protected by extreme acts of violence. He said that the outlawing of certain legal highs had steadily pushed the business underground and created a criminal underclass on Guernsey. As he talked, Bobby clinically packed legal highs into sealed bags that would then be distributed to users all over the island and beyond.

'A lot of legal highs are now shipped through Guernsey,' explained Bobby. 'This place has been like a hub for the stuff. The authorities were so wrong to clamp down on illegal drugs in the first place. That left a gap that legal highs have now filled. Even today, the island's government stupidly thinks they can kill off the legal-highs trade just by banning them. If they'd had more experience with real drugs they would have realized that it just doesn't work like that.'

Bobby continued: 'Legal highs turned up here in the first place because young people were intrigued. There is now an enormous demand here and that isn't going to just die out.'

The core of Bobby's business is buying in large shipments of legal highs and then 'turning them around' very quickly by selling them on to the UK, Western Europe and beyond. 'The key is to turn around the product very quickly. That's obviously good for profit margins but it's also vital when it comes to this stuff. I like to know that before Guernsey has time to ban a substance I've already moved it on.

'It's ironic to talk like this because it's exactly the same principle as illegal drugs. All the richest gangsters are the ones who buy huge shipments and then sell them on very quickly. The less time you have in possession of the actual stuff the less risk to your own liberty.'

Bobby was born and brought up on Guernsey and he insisted that was another reason why he was able to operate without any major interference. He explained: 'I keep my profile low but my family has good connections within the Guernsey police. They know I run this business but they have made it known to me that they will not bust me as long as I quickly move the produce on abroad. But if they had any idea some of my legal highs were consumed here then they'd come down on me like a ton of bricks.'

Bobby continued: 'That's the risky bit for me and to tell you the truth I think I may pull out of selling here altogether because the exporting side of my business has taken off so well that I don't need the relative chicken-feed income from selling legal highs here.'

Bobby said he also imported and exported silk scarves and Persian rugs and that has helped camouflage the bulk of his legal-high business. 'I'm not a fool and I certainly have never wanted to rub anyone's faces in what I am doing, so it makes sense to keep the rest of my business pottering along nicely.'

He explained: 'Essentially, I'm just a very hard-working guy who is making a decent living. I like to keep to myself and I don't want anyone else knowing what I'm doing because then I would be dead meat in all sorts of different ways.'

Bobby refused to introduce me directly to anyone else involved in legal highs on Guernsey, so I 'recruited' a local 'guide' called Jimmy in order to go further into the island's darkest corners.

As I began exploring the island's legal-high hinterlands, I discovered a community of youngsters who get off their faces on these manufactured psychotropics virtually every night of the week.

It was 8 p.m. at the end of a glorious spring day and the sun was slowly going down beyond the rippling sea as Jimmy and I approached a group of misty-eyed teenagers sitting at the far end of a sandy beach. We were in a relatively deserted corner of this unusual, over-populated island that remains somewhat overshadowed by its reputation as one of the world's tax havens.

But you wouldn't believe it from the expression on the faces of these teenagers. Their parents were all wealthy middle-class citizens but they themselves were in their own words 'bored out of our tiny brains on this fucking dull island'.

No wonder legal highs have thrived on places like Guernsey where illegal drugs have in the past failed to make an impact, and it is a similar story in many rural areas of the UK. Today there is a whole new generation discovering exotic substances for the first time. Numerous groups of fed-up youngsters feeling trapped in a society that prides itself on being *behind* the times have finally found something that gives them a way out.

The first psychonaut I talked to was Lenny. He was seventeen years old and had dropped out of school a year earlier. 'There's nothing to do here. But unfortunately for our parents – who come from this island – they never got a chance to experiment with drugs because there were none whatsoever here until legal highs appeared on the scene.'

Lenny reckoned that if his parents had known a bit more about drugs, they might have been a bit less hysterical about the new breed of narcotics that have flooded into the island in recent years. 'My parents are not cool about this. They look on all drugs, both legal and illegal, as evil and they have no idea why anyone would want to take them. It's made the atmosphere at home really heavy ever since my mum found some legal highs under my mattress.

'That's why so many of us now meet at places like this because our parents have forced us out. They don't want us doing this stuff at home. It's not a good situation at all. Very sad in many ways. D'you know that for more than a year, my mum and dad just thought I was addicted to being on my laptop in my bedroom when all the time I was taking legal highs?

'Now they're trying to ban them after finally waking up to their use because of so many problems among the island's young. That's also forced us to get high together here on the beach because it's nice to hang out together and not have to be shouted and screamed at all the time.'

Some Guernsey inhabitants believe that the island's 'tough love' approach to legal-highs users has helped turn parts of this quintessential piece of Middle England into a virtual ghetto.

Lenny's friend Carla explained: 'So what if we like to get

high? There isn't much else to do here, is there? My dad ran off with a younger woman last year and went to live on the mainland and that sent me a bit over the edge.

'I found myself cooped up with my mum. She was in tears most of the time and, sure, I felt sorry for her and for the first six months after my dad left I did everything to try and help my mum. But I needed an outlet for myself and when I started taking legal highs I realized just how good it felt to escape all the problems of my world for a few hours.

'My mum had no idea what I was up to at first because I tended to go and stay at my friend Casey's house some nights just to get a break from Mum. That's when we started smoking Spice. It was amazing. It left me feeling floaty and happy and content for the first time in my life.

'Then we went out to a party at a friend's house and some-one gave me some speedy stuff called MMDA or something like that. It was out of this world. I discovered "places" I'd never been before. I know that part of the reason I like these legal highs is because of what I've been through at home, but I can honestly say that it's no surprise so many kids round here take them.'

Carla continued: 'It really pisses me off that adults seem to think we're no better than heroin addicts. They just don't get it. We're chilling out. Our futures look pretty boring – even frightening – ahead of us and we need something to get us through this stage of our lives.'

Carla then admitted that she'd decided to come clean to her mother about her use of legal highs. 'She said she was heartbroken when I told her I was taking this stuff. I tried to explain that it was no different to her drinking a bottle of wine each night, which is what she has done since my dad left us. But she will not have it. She says I've let her down and I'm really scared that soon the atmosphere at home will get so bad that I'll have to leave. I know my mum is upset about Dad dumping her but she's not thinking about what I'm going through as well as her. I need an outlet otherwise my life feels as if it's not worth living. Is that so hard to understand?'

Then I met another member of this group of legal-high dopers called Jamie. He was just sixteen years old but believed he'd be taking such substances for the rest of his life. He explained: 'Until I discovered legal highs I didn't have a proper life here. Honestly, it was that bad. Then I heard about this guy down in St Peter Port who supplied all sorts of legal highs.

'He assured me that everything he sold had been personally tested by him and his mates, so I bought some. It would be great if there was a head shop here on Guernsey but there's no way they'd allow one to open. So we have no choice but to use a dealer. The Internet is too risky because it leaves a footprint and most of us still want to try and hide all this from our parents.'

Jamie and his friends told of dealers who regularly changed phone numbers to avoid the authorities. 'Sure, they're legal but most people here on the island would inform on you to the police if they knew you were using them,' said Jamie. 'It's not as if we're scoring off a man on a street corner. We know this guy. His family knows my family. It's better that way because we both know we've got to keep quiet.'

Meanwhile Jamie's friend Lenny said he believed that the designer drug problem on Guernsey was still going to get a lot worse. He explained: 'This is just the tip of the iceberg, man. There're thousands of kids like us on this island who want to use legal highs and most of them are going to try them at some time or other.

'Inside schools pupils talk about legal highs all the time and swap experiences on what are the best ones. Instead of outlawing the products and making all of us feel like criminals they should embrace the use of such things and allow it to be done out in the open. That way we'd all get through that stage of our lives with little hassle and most of us would then move onto safe, secure jobs with 2.1 children and a semi. I'm joking but there is a serious point behind what I'm saying.

'If you push this scene too far underground you create many more problems in the long term. They're called legal highs because they're legal. What people use them for is up to them, surely? We're all supposedly intelligent human beings. Why can't we just do what we want? We're not harming anyone else.'

The following day, I walked into a bar in St Peter Port and discovered that legal highs were, indeed, available beyond the Internet. My guide Jimmy was offered a brand-new equivalent of cocaine from a man who approached us as we stood supping on our drinks. It was a bizarre experience to be offered a legal high in this way.

Later Jimmy explained: 'A lot of the kids out here taking legal highs are so scared of being arrested that they avoid the Internet like the plague because it leaves a record of a transaction. In any case, a lot of these kids only use cash. So here, dealers often pop up in bars and pubs because they know that people often want a legal high at short notice once they've had a few drinks and are "in the mood".'

But Guernsey's legal-high 'scene' is not just the domain of teenagers. An older, richer crowd are also taking a wide range of designer drugs. And, surprisingly, their motivation for turning to legal highs on Guernsey is much the same as those younger users.

CHAPTER 29

DEL

'I'm bored shitless by my life out here,' explained Del, twenty-seven. He's been 'trapped' on Guernsey ever since his billionaire banker father decided to become a tax exile from the UK and divorce his wife at the same time. 'Every day is the same to me,' said Del. 'Legal highs are my only enjoyment out here. When we first moved here three years ago, I was distraught because I'd been used to buying cocaine in London as easily as a pint of lager. I knew that those sort of drugs were really hard to come by in Guernsey. But then I discovered legal highs.'

At least four times a week, Del gets in his shiny new BMW and heads over to an area of Guernsey known, confusingly, as 'the island' because it is a stretch of beach with a handful of modest, by Guernsey standards, one-storey houses right opposite a small island. There, Del and his friends buy their legal highs from a dealer. Often they stay with him and kick back and smoke Spice, the nearest thing to cannabis they can obtain on Guernsey, but it's clearly just as addictive. Del admits he's hooked and can't get enough of the stuff.

'At weekends I mainly do the coke-type legal highs to give me bursts of energy but Spice in the week helps me drift through the boredom perfectly.'

Del's billionaire father is so concerned by his son's addiction problems that he has twice sent him to drug recovery clinics back on the UK mainland. 'But they don't help much. It's strange really to end up being surrounded by illegal drug addicts when all you've taken is a bit of harmless stuff – because that's what I feel about legal highs.

'My father didn't know what else to do except throw loads of money at my problem. I hated it in those clinics, partly because I didn't feel I belonged there and also because the people were such losers. I don't consider myself to be a loser. Sure, I took and still take too much stuff but it's not as if I can't afford it, is it? My dad forced me to come and live here because he reckoned it would keep me away from the bad crowd who were feeding me illegal drugs when we lived in the Home Counties.

'At first when we arrived here I got quite suicidal with the boredom. My dad chucked me a big allowance, safe in the knowledge that I couldn't spend it on drugs any more because there were none on Guernsey. Then along came legal highs. For about a year, my father had no idea they even existed. He was travelling a lot on business and I'd order them in while he was away. I got a kind of kick out of the fact he thought I was straight and sober while the opposite was true.'

But there were side-effects to some of the legal highs that Del was taking. 'I'm a pretty over-the-top character and I tend not to just dabble at things and legal highs were something I threw myself into with great energy. I tried just about everything that was out there and a lot of times I did it on my own in the house because my father was away so much.'

Then one day, Del's father arrived home early from a business trip. 'He turned up one afternoon where I was tripping on some acid-type legal high. I was off my head and when he walked in through the front door I actually thought I was imagining it. My dad's face dropped and he knew pretty quickly that I was on something.

'He told me later he already had his suspicions because he'd noticed how much weight I'd lost and how grey and gaunt I looked in the face. I was so stoned I couldn't even speak, so he sent me to my room where I proceeded to have a really bad trip and the next morning he went completely apeshit at me and insisted I go to a clinic in Gloucestershire that afternoon.

'His secretary booked a private plane and twenty-four hours later I was sitting there with a bunch of heroin addicts telling them my experiences with legal highs. I was such an amateur compared to them. I felt as if they were all laughing at me under their breaths. I hated it in that place and checked myself out after three days but then I discovered my dad had cancelled my credit cards and I couldn't even afford to pay for a flight back to Guernsey. Obviously I hadn't told my dad what I'd done. I tried to contact my mother but she didn't want to know because by this time she had a new husband and a new family and I was not part of her life any more.

'Virtually destitute, I slept on a park bench the first night after I checked out of the clinic. It was horrible and very lonely. Eventually, I plucked up the courage to call my father and tell him what I'd done. He was surprisingly reasonable and immediately got me booked on a flight back here. But you know what? I wish my dad had just cut me loose there and then. I would have had to fend for myself but instead I got back into my gilded cage where I've remained ever since.

'No wonder I've drifted back to using legal highs. I try not to do them in the house, which is partly why I go to the "island" where a lot of older legal-high users come on beautiful sunny evenings like tonight. I want to kick back and relax. Okay, I know I'm a lot luckier than most to have all my dad's money behind me but in some ways it really is a curse.

'My life is now so regimented it's quite bizarre. I get up in the morning usually late at about ten or eleven and then I hang out with my dad for a bit if he's here. Then I go back into my section of the house and start playing games on the computer. If my father is out by then I try and persuade a friend to come over. If Dad is around then I stay in my room for most of the rest of the day. It's not a very healthy existence, especially not for someone of my age.'

Del said he was resigned to spending the rest of his life on Guernsey. 'My dad has made it clear that he'll keep financing my life as long as I stay here, so I don't really have a choice. The trouble is that the longer I'm here the more entrenched I become in this easy life. I'm putting on a lot of weight again and I'm finding it harder and harder to interact with most people because I have so little to say.

'There is a side to me that would probably be much happier if I was arrested and then slung into jail. Then I could push my dad into disinheriting me or something like that and then he'd have to cut me loose. But the trouble is that I've become a very lazy person. I don't want to go to work like everyone else.'

Del's closest friends are both the sons of other billionaire businessmen on Guernsey. 'It's no surprise that we've been drawn together because we all suffer in the same way. Drugs, whether legal or illegal, thrive on boredom and we are classic examples of this. Add to this the fact that we have access to money whenever we want it and we really are prime candidates for full-scale drug addiction.'

Del has even toyed with the idea of starting to trade in designer drugs himself. 'I need to get my teeth into something and I really thought it was booming so much that it might be a great starter business. But my father didn't see the funny side of it. He likes to keep up appearances here on Guernsey and he hates to rock the boat in case it causes him any problems because of his tax-exile status.

'So just the very thought of his only child being involved

in such a dodgy business scared the shit out of him. Not surprisingly, he ended up coming down on me like the proverbial ton of bricks for even suggesting such a plan. I tried to laugh it off as a joke but I think he knew perfectly well I was being deadly serious.'

Today, Del continues to wrestle with his self-confessed addiction to a number of legal-high substances and he said he had reached a dangerous crossroads in his life. 'I feel as if my life has just seized up. I can't seem to do anything except take legal highs to try and water down the state I'm in. It's a horrible situation. I'm trapped here on Guernsey. Apart from taking legal highs, there is no reason to get up in the morning.

'My life feels completely pointless and I'm being more and more reclusive. Even when my father is here I sometimes don't see him for days on end. At the age of twenty-seven I'm more like an angry, moody teenager hiding in his room most of the day because he cannot face the outside world.

'None of this can be blamed on legal highs, either. If I'd chosen this path for myself then at least it would have been my decision. But even that has been taken out of my hands by my dad. I need to escape from here but I cannot survive without his money. I'm in what best could be described as a classic conundrum. I just wish I could come up with a way to fix my life.'

CHAPTER 30

THE FALLA CLAN

The Falla family are said to have Guernsey flowing through their blood. At least three generations of them have lived on the island and Michael, the current head of the clan, worked for twenty-five years as a policeman. But then in 2012, Guernsey's gilded middle-class inhabitants were rocked by the revelation that Michael Falla and his family had been running a lucrative designer drug business for many years. After a series of failed business ventures and the loss of the family home due to financial difficulties, they'd begun importing mephedrone and carried on smuggling the drug after it was banned in 2010. They first came under suspicion when, during a search of the family's home on a completely unrelated matter, the police discovered a stun gun, pepper spray and batons in their son, Charles's bedroom. While the police were in the house Charles's mother Mandy asked where the money was, which led officers to search the bedroom again. They found almost £8,000 in cash, which the family said was earnings from the father's job as a taxi driver.

It later emerged that more than 1,500 legal-high tablets had been imported through the post, directly to the family home or to another property. A package, containing mephedrone tablets, was then intercepted by police in May 2011 and its contents swapped. That dummy replacement package enabled Guernsey Border Agency officers to trace it to Charles Falla, who was taken into custody.

The majority of these pills were LU Dove mephedrone tablets acquired from a contact in the neighbouring Channel Island of Jersey known as Mr X. Although initially the Falla parents had restricted their involvement to looking after the operation's finances – laundering the cash and paying off their supplier – after Charles was arrested they took a more hands-on role in the business. The fact that their son was behind bars was not, it seems, sufficient warning for them to stop.

Finally, in July 2011, Customs officers intercepted Mr and Mrs Falla when they arrived on the island on a car ferry from St Malo. A sniffer dog discovered they'd concealed more than 1.5 kg of synthetic cannabinoids, similar to cannabis resin, in their car doors. The border agency estimated the street value of all the drugs at somewhere between £258,000 and £344,000.

Family members were eventually jailed for almost twenty-eight years by Guernsey's Royal Court for importing 'legal highs' worth more than £250,000. Michael, sixty-eight, his wife Mandy, fifty-one, and their sons Charles, twenty, and Alex, eighteen, pleaded guilty to a variety of charges including importing drugs and money laundering. Michael and Mandy were each jailed for eight years. Charles and Alex were given youth detention, eight years and three years eight months respectively. Both sons admitted to conspiracy to supply drugs, while Charles was also charged with importing mephedrone, by then classified as a Class B drug on the island after it was outlawed in 2010.

Judge Dame Heather Steel told the Guernsey court at the Falla hearing: 'It funded the family lifestyle at a time when no one in the family had another legitimate form of employment.' In passing sentence Judge Steel told the Falla parents: 'Neither provide any reason or accepted any responsibility . . . your attitude to the proceedings in this court was of arrogance to your current situation. You assisted and encouraged your son Charles. [It's] incredible that you continued to be involved when your family was being investigated and your son Charles was in custody. Misfortune can never be an excuse for criminal activity.' The judge told Michael Falla he was once a 'distinguished member of the community' whose career had 'ended in disgrace' and the 'destruction of your family'.

The island of Guernsey perfectly highlighted the problems that occur when legal highs grip a community. But there are many other examples too.

In Scotland, a new front has opened up in the so-called war on drugs thanks to the influx of legal highs, which have introduced an even more lucrative element into the narcotics trade and undoubtedly added to law enforcement confusion.

Experts in Scotland believe that legal highs are being forced underground by legislation outlawing certain substances and the only real losers are the taxmen. As one street dealer in Edinburgh told me: 'A lot of people actually get a thrill out of scoring drugs as well as taking them. Legal highs seemed a bit of a soft option at first because there was no risk element involved in getting them. Now they've been pushed further underground, dealers are once again becoming an integral part of the process.'

In 2012, at least 320 Scots were taken to hospital after experimenting with legal highs, and it's claimed that at least three people in Scotland die each month from taking them. But the dealers and their market continue to move quicker than the law ever can. It's hard to fight a war when the names of the actual substances change with alarming regularity.

One of Scotland's most senior police officers, Detective Chief Superintendent John Cuddihy, argued: 'There is too much focus on the words "legal" and "illegal". Let's focus on the harm these substances cause.'

Scottish police chiefs have conceded they've 'encouraged' the head shops selling legal highs to leave town centres, where they are considered a stain on the community. Chief Inspector Gordon Milne from Arbroath police said: 'We're aware of the issue of legal highs, and we're working to see if there's any methods of best educating our young people about not getting into this business.'

Mr Milne said he was aware of the online groups such as Arbroath Against Legal Highs, which gained over 1,800 supporters in the first month it was launched.

A Scottish Drugs Forum spokeswoman said: 'Legal highs can be a particular problem in rural areas due to reduced access to other drugs. Head shops actually represent a relatively small portion of legal-high sales, but they draw attention because of their visibility. The trouble is that prohibition can sometimes drive a trade underground.'

Legal-high users in Scotland come in all sorts of surprising shapes and sizes. Darren, thirty-eight, and Jonathan, forty-one, fit the *Trainspotting* profile well: bored, disillusioned men who began experimenting with street drugs in late adolescence, before being hit hard by the influx of heroin into Edinburgh. They both stay away from smack now, but have an entirely different relationship with legal highs such as tranquillizers and the now-banned sedative 6-APB (or Benzo Fury). They deal only to close friends but insisted in an article published in *Men's Health* magazine that the risks of taking these substances was minimal.

'No one I know who's used drugs would argue that these new ones are stronger or more addictive than heroin or crack,' Darren told *Men's Health*. 'But they are "new" – and that's really the point. If a pill that's only been around for ten minutes can knock someone like me sideways, that has ten years' experience of using heavy, illegal drugs, on a daily basis, then that's . . . unusual.'

Darren agreed that so-called 'fake cannabis' such as Spice can spark extremely strong hallucinations. It's acknowledged among users that even those products that are marketed as supposedly chilling you out can instead prompt hallucinations or palpitations. According to Jonathan, one of the reasons why more and more people were turning to legal highs was the falling purity of regular narcotics. 'There's so little actual heroin in a bag today that you might as well be addicted to brick-dust,' he said.

Many users, suppliers and even law enforcement officers believe the legal highs in Scotland are often much more potent than old-fashioned illicit drugs. 'Cocaine here is twenty per cent pure at the most,' one local addiction worker told *Men's Health* magazine. 'Guys who're used to those illegal drugs take a larger amount of the legal equivalent, expecting less of an effect. But the legal drug is probably about ninety per cent pure,' he said. And most important of all, they cost about half as much to buy.

One drug, methiopropamine, otherwise known as Charly Sheen on the legal-high market, is 'selling like hotcakes' to junkies in Scotland, according to one expert. 'That's because it's incredibly similar to another much-studied drug called methamphetamine – that's crystal meth to you and me.'

In Edinburgh, on the front line of this foggy war on drugs, Jonathan and Darren described to *Men's Health* how legal highs have made such an impact. They claimed there were people injecting mephedrone sometimes up to forty times a day. And in order to do this they had to use syringes four times the size of any heroin addict's. Jonathan explained: 'I've seen friends taken in for emergency psychiatric tests within a few weeks of heavy use [of mephedrone].' It's scary stuff.

Not surprisingly, a number of powerful criminals have begun to emerge from this legal-high netherworld.

One of the most notorious among these is a man called Gary Hewitt, who has so far proved untouchable to the authorities, according to an exposé on him that ran in the *Daily Record*. He's said to be a legal-high kingpin who recruits dealers with a promise of £100,000 a year and police are convinced his business is thriving. The police even admit they're powerless to stop him, despite at least three deaths being linked to the substances he produces.

Hewitt was the victim of a newspaper sting when a

reporter was sold six grams of a legal high. Then he was dubbed 'The dealer behind Scotland's biggest network of deadly new party drugs.'

Like so many other career criminals trading the latest breed of synthetic narcotics, this 31-year-old believes he's safe from arrest because he's selling products that are – according to the letter of the law – legal. It's difficult to know how much money Hewitt really makes but it is clear that he's a major player in the Scottish legal-high game.

Hewitt boasted to Scottish journalists of raking in huge profits from all over Scotland. He attributed this to being a canny operator. Hewitt realized that if he was greedy and tried to charge the same amount as people were paying for cocaine, he'd face an uphill struggle. 'The beauty of legal highs is that they are much cheaper than illegal drugs.' Hewitt said the most important element of his 'business' was 'having a good client base'. Even if it meant that he ended up giving heavy discounts to people who bought in bulk he knew he was still guaranteed to make money hand over fist. Hewitt provided journalists with a price list with projected profit margins, and offered to sell six grams of K'Kane for £100. He explained: 'You'll love it. You'll see how good it is and then you'll be back for more.' Hewitt was obviously confident of his product's appeal. At one point in the interview he asserted that he'd been to parties where he'd been told that people preferred his K'Kane – a white powder he asserts stimulates the same effects as cocaine – to the coke they usually bought. Apparently even other dealers were praising its quality. He was also aware that there was a danger that some people might go a bit overboard when it came to taking K'Kane. 'I had to stop selling to one woman because she was buying every day and was completely wasted.' The same woman ended up in debt to Hewitt, but he believed that 'folk like her are few and far between'.

At one stage Hewitt opened a head shop in Glasgow but the police forced him to shut it down. His products flew off the shelves, finding an especially enthusiastic market among the city's students. He knew that because he was sticking to the letter of the law the police had no grounds to put a stop to this roaring trade. However, the authorities got round this by putting his landlord under heavy pressure. Hewitt wasn't disheartened, even when his landlord eventually gave in. He realized that he could make even more money by advertising over the Internet, especially since selling online cuts out costly overheads like rent. He advertises K'Kane along with Benzo Fury, one of the drugs that replaced the outlawed mephedrone, on his Facebook page and was able to run his dodgy business from his home, which is just a stone's throw from where one teenage girl died after taking a substance called K-CAT.

Hewitt's story illustrates the profound and complicated ethical and moral questions that those people who produce and sell legal highs face. Many of them must know that their products have the potential to cause considerable damage, even death to users, so how do they rationalize this risk? One common response was articulated by another Scottish legal-high magnate: 'The same question could be levelled at alcohol, or at cars. Does the car manufacturer feel guilty when people are killed by cars? People are safe as long as they are used within the guidelines given.'

Wales is yet another corner of the United Kingdom that is facing a serious legal-high epidemic. Criminals in Wales are proving to be just as adept as elsewhere at making the kind of minor tweaks to banned substances that allow them to stay a knife-edge ahead of the law.

Many of the new psychotropics are derivatives of mephedrone, but this 'family' similarity doesn't make it any easier for the British legal system to analyse and classify the abundance of new chemical drugs being produced. The proliferation of these substances is on a scale outside the experience of even veteran law enforcement officers.

The incremental changes made by increasingly sophisticated operations mean that it's enormously hard for the police to establish whether they're facing an illegal psychoactive, a drug that's in the process of being criminalized, or a perfectly legal substance. For instance, one of the most common legal highs to have been on the market in Wales in recent years was NRG-2, which was a modification of another chemical compound, NRG-1, that had been recommended for classification as a Class B drug in 2010. And NRG-1 was itself adapted from mephedrone.

So it's no surprise that one legal-high supplier on the Web based in South Wales felt able to brazenly advertise a 'mephedrone replacement'. Selling the product at £15 a gram, the supplier even promised same day delivery to local areas including Newport, Cardiff and Blaenau Gwent.

Welshman Eddie is middle class, has a well-paid job in marketing but makes a 'half decent' secondary income flogging legal highs on the Internet from his suburban semi-detached home on the outskirts of Cardiff. Eddie started out buying legal highs for his friends, who were fed up with being ripped off by illegal drug dealers. He quickly realized legal highs would make a 'decent little sideline'. Eddie quickly built up such a large database of customers that he was tempted to quit his day job but he said that his instincts told him not to take the plunge and, as a result, he's now one of the busiest 'amateur' legal-high dealers in Wales.

'When you talk to most people over the age of forty, they haven't got a clue what legal highs are,' said Eddie. 'Legal highs seem to have created a marketplace all of their own. They're not just about replacing illegal drugs. They have their own marketplace and that means they're hopefully here to stay.'

Eddie reckons there are many others inside the legal-high business who hold down a normal nine-to-five job as well. Eddie explained: 'These days with stagnant wages, people often need to have two jobs. I work in marketing and I also deal in legal highs. It's a good combination because I can sort out all my Internet sales each evening when I get home and I'm very careful to keep both jobs completely separate.'

Eddie also has a wife and two young children at home to support. 'Most people think of legal-high dealers as young dopers sitting drooping over their laptops making a few bob here and there but this business is deadly serious to me. I have a family to support and they are my main priority.'

Eddie is also an unusual legal high 'dealer' in another way because he only deals in approved legal highs. He explained: 'I'm a law-abiding citizen so I make sure that all the products you can buy on my website are 100 per cent legal. Now it can be quite difficult to keep up with all the new laws when it comes to legal highs but I am obsessed with obeying the word of the law because I have a responsibility to my family and I promised my wife I would not put them at risk in any way.'

Eddie asserted that one of the main reasons why he insisted on selling only approved legal highs was the death of a school friend from illegal drugs. He explained: 'One of my best friends died from a heroin overdose when we were sixteen. It devastated me and scared me off drugs for a long time. I couldn't understand why anyone would want to take something that might kill them. It just didn't make sense.'

So Eddie set up a specialised legal-high site. But like all legal-high dealers and suppliers, he still insisted on not being identified for this book. 'There's a lot of stigma attached to legal highs where I live,' he explained. 'Parents are convinced they're just as dangerous as illegal drugs and I don't want a situation where my family are smeared because I'm doing this as a sideline. It's much better if most people don't know about it.'

PART SIX

HEAD SHOPS

I remember seeing dragons and spikes . . .
A Kent college student shortly before he had
a heart attack in his bedroom after smoking
the synthetic cannabis drug in a bong after
buying it at his local head shop

Kent is known to many as the Garden of England. Its rolling fields of golden corn, converted millhouses and luscious green pastures have made it a picture-postcard corner of the UK. Its peaceful, winding country lanes are filled with modest folk whose love of gardening is about as close as many of them would ever get to some of the so-called 'plant foods' passed off as legal highs. But lurking in among the historic villages and towns of Kent are more so-called head shops supplying legal highs than any other county in the UK.

But then again, at one end of Kent are the Channel ports of Dover and Folkestone, which provide a gateway in and out of Europe and all its highly lucrative drug-trafficking routes.

For there is another side to Kent. There are urban areas which have long been privately labelled 'The Wild West' by police because of the lawless society which exists beneath this county's otherwise respectable veneer. One of the biggest clues is the disproportionately large number of immaculate mock-Tudor mansions with long driveways, high brick walls, sophisticated closed circuit TV, electronically operated gates and a couple of Rottweilers on duty. One notorious villain called his dogs 'Brinks' and 'Mat' after one of his most infamous criminal enterprises and even had centrally heated kennels specially built for them.

These well-heeled citizens often describe themselves as 'businessmen' and 'property developers' but an increasing number of them are only dealing in legal highs these days.

Add to that the vast number of head shops in Kent and you have a combustible legal-high mix. Critics say the head shops pose a risk to health because many of these stores stock designer drugs with a record of landing people in hospital. There have already been several deaths in Kent over the last few years linked to legal highs, but the warnings don't seem to have been heeded.

Kent police insist the head shops should openly recognize the impact of the products they're selling. One officer explained: 'They all have a massive responsibility and I don't see any evidence that they're taking that responsibility seriously – how could they when there have been no tests on the health risks of these drugs? So they just have to go through this absurd double-think where they have to sell stuff which they know is dangerous.'

The shelves of most head shops are filled with paraphernalia such as pipes and bongs used for smoking cannabis, alongside the scales and 'stench-proof' plastic bags popular with dealers. Behind the counter are displays of luridly packaged sachets of products with names like Amsterdam Gold, Herbal Bush and Mayan Dream.

A shop assistant in one head shop I visited coolly ran

through the vast selection of drugs on sale in his store. The names he mentioned ran into dozens of pills, powders and 'smokes', all packaged in gaudy wrapping and apparently containing substances that were 'close relatives' of those illegal drug legends coke, Ecstasy, ketamine, and even LSD.

The assistant couldn't have been more charming. He made it clear he had tried the majority of the products himself and sounded almost proud of his experiences with legal highs. Head shops are providing the perfect one-stop shopping experience for anyone wanting to try a legal high. No grubby street corners talking to dodgy-looking dealers who whisper out of the corner of their mouths. No, this was the 2014 version. Clean produce supplied with a smile and a promise that 'all credit cards are accepted'.

It's no big surprise that cannabis-like legal highs are so popular with teenagers. In head shops they cost around the same as half a pint of bitter. Their packaging might stay well away from ever mentioning 'weed', 'hash' or 'marijuana', but with names that mention 'leaves', 'high' and other key words, it's blatantly obvious what market they're looking to compete in.

The head-shop assistant said: 'These are the real deal. I reckon they work better than hash and skunk. You get a much stronger high and it's more interestin', if you know what I mean. Some people come in here saying they want somethin' mellow to smoke and I tell them to stick to the real stuff because this smoke blows yer mind.'

What he didn't reveal was that no one has ever worked

out what damage this stuff can do to your health and life expectancy.

Elsewhere in the UK, there has been a backlash against head shops. In the city of Plymouth, in the West of England, owners of head shops have been suffering repeated vandalism and even violent assaults in the aftermath of deaths allegedly linked to legal highs. Vigilante parents were initially blamed for the attacks in June 2013, but another, even more sinister 'element' has been implicated. Some of these traders believe that illicit drug dealers have paid youngsters to firebomb and vandalize premises because the existence of legal highs has hit their profits from cocaine, hash and heroin.

The attacks seem to have been provoked after it was reported that seizures of mephedrone in Plymouth, known by its street name 'Bubble', had gone from 4,646 grams between April 2011 and March 2012 to 5,405 grams between April 2012 and March 2013.

Owners of the city's half a dozen head shops insisted in the local media that their products were not responsible for any local deaths associated with legal-high consumption. The shop owners also claimed police regularly raided their stores and confiscated thousands of pounds' worth of legal highs, which were never returned even though they did not break the law. 'We're all running honest, legitimate businesses,' said one trader. 'We pay our taxes and openly trade in legal highs without any subterfuge. We can't help the cowboys out there on the Internet, who're giving us a bad name.'

Another head-shop owner in Plymouth claimed that he'd been 'visited' by local gangsters who 'suggested' his premises would be damaged if he did not pay them a 'fee'. He recalled: 'They were after protection money because they said they needed to make up for all the lost income they were suffering because more kids take legal highs here in Plymouth than consume all the traditional illegal drugs.'

In Northern Ireland, head shops are being blamed for the booming sales of legal highs. Shops selling substances over the counter are drawing young people into the drug scene in bigger numbers and at an earlier age, according to the Forum for Action on Substance Abuse (Fasa). 'The introduction of legal highs has made drugs far more accessible to younger people,' according to Alex Bunting, an official with the charity. We always had the issue of illicit drugs but since legal highs have come in, we have seen something new in terms of usage levels and age of onset.'

Alex Bunting continued: 'If you think about cannabis, Ecstasy or even cocaine, human beings have used these drugs for a long time, so we know what the side-effects are. The downside of legal highs is that none of them have been put through a test. We work with clients, hardened illicit drug users, and they say they get a better, more potent hit off legal highs.'

Owen O'Neill from Northern Ireland's Public Health

Agency said the rise in shops selling legal highs in the province meant access to dangerous substances was now greater than ever. 'The head shops present a challenge to us all in terms of a route for young people getting their hands on drugs as opposed to approaching dealers who young people may not know how to access.'

CHAPTER 31

BEN

Ben runs a high-street head shop renowned as a local meeting place for youngsters, which specializes in legal highs and other drug paraphernalia in a quiet English south coast town. You'd imagine it would be fine to identify Ben by his real name because he's in charge of what he insisted was a perfectly legal business. But when I entered his premises and tried to organize an interview it was as hard as door-stepping a bank robber in the badlands of South London.

You see, Ben is obsessed with secrecy. He explained: 'Undercover coppers come in here all the time trying to catch us out. I have to be very careful and there is no point in rubbing the police's noses in it otherwise they'd soon close us down.'

Ben runs the head shop on behalf of an older man who owns the franchise to three similar shops along the same

253

strip of coastline. But then youths in these quiet towns don't have much else to do other than experiment with drugs. Ben explained: 'Yeah, many of the kids round here have little chance of a decent job, so it's no big surprise that they like getting high, is it? I used to be just the same. I wanted to work and live in a big city like London but I could never afford the move, so I stuck around here getting off my head until I was lucky enough to meet Dermot, who owns this shop, and his two other business partners.'

As Ben spoke to me, a regular came in and bought a bag of NIS 50 – synthetic cannabis. Ben pocketed the cash and wrote down the purchase on a notepad. He insisted the store kept records for tax purposes. Ben admitted that the herb he sells doesn't give the same high as the real stuff and can sometimes give you a headache. Still, he says, people have grown to like it and prefer to know they won't get arrested – a fact he believes probably won't change any time soon.

Ben explained: 'I think they [police] want it to be like this. They know that if one day they really, really come out and close down all these shops, they're just going to sell it in the streets or alleys. It's not going to go away.'

The spread of head shops throughout the south-east of England is pretty phenomenal. Yet many of them are run very discreetly to try and avoid attracting the attention of the police.

Ben explained: 'I thought you was a copper the moment you walked in here because you don't get many people in here who're over thirty. The police are really sneaky. They want to catch us offering substances that have been outlawed and they've got it in their heads that we're no better than street-corner drug dealers.

'It's very unfair because my boss Dermot is incredibly careful not to stock anything that could be classified as illegal. If anything does get quickly outlawed we dump it. Luckily we never order huge amounts of anything although many of the suppliers are constantly trying to pressurize us to buy big orders, probably because they know they're about to get lumbered with huge amounts of a duff, out of date product.'

Ben says that he is 'forbidden' from recommending any product in the shop because virtually all of it is clearly labelled 'not fit for human consumption or something similar'. He went on: 'It's a bleedin' joke, isn't it? But there is no way I would say to anyone who came in here that one of these products was worth a try. It would be more than my job is worth. I know it sounds a bit daft to run a shop where you can't actually recommend the products but that is the way it is.'

The head-shop business in the UK has been booming since 2010 and it's reckoned that by the end of 2015 there will be approximately 500 such stores throughout Britain bringing in an annual income of around £100 million. 'I think there'll come a time when the police and other authorities will have to come to terms with what we sell and allow us to behave and operate like the rest of the shops on Britain's high streets,' said Ben.

Ironically, the town centres where the legal-high shops really flourish are the rundown ones that have been hit by the Internet revolution. Ben explained: 'You see, they can't exactly refuse to let us open for trade because they need our business and our rent desperately to help inject a bit of life into rundown high streets like this one.'

There must be hundreds if not thousands of similar locations all over the country in need of the sort of business a head shop can bring. The rents are very low so not surprisingly it makes it an attractive proposition for legal-high sellers.

The recurring theme I came across while researching this book was that despite the supposed Internet revolution, many consumers preferred to deal with real people in a real setting when it comes to purchasing and consuming legal highs.

'Yeah, that's a weird one, ain't it?' said Ben. 'You'd have thought all those kids sitting at home on their laptops would be ordering up legal highs by the lorryload but you forget something very important; if they ordered the stuff online it would be posted to their homes and then their mums and dads would know what they were up to. Also, they want this stuff to come recommended by *real* human beings like me.

'By coming in here, they're avoiding all that potential hassle at home. You see, most of our customers ask a lot of questions. As I said I have to be careful what I say but if they just want to know that certain things are all right to take then I try and give them the nod. I guess in many ways we're the one-stop shop to pick up the produce they've already tried to educate themselves about online.'

Ben, with his multiple piercings and tattoos, might look like a bit of a cliché but he is far from stupid. 'I've learned to be very careful in this business. Discretion is vital and while I might look like a bit of a mug, I can assure you I am not. I'm not going to admit even to you that I do recommend certain products. I'll just leave that to your imagination.'

Ben claimed that two young undercover policemen had come into his head shop only the previous week trying to trick him into recommending a legal high. 'I knew what they were up to the moment they came in here. Both of them were very healthy looking – not a good sign – and their eyes darted around the shop nonstop. They seemed shifty and I watched them carefully through the security screen before I even stepped out of the back of the shop to go behind the counter. Stupid arseholes then started calling me "dude", which is always a bit of a giveaway.'

But worse was to come. Ben explained: 'One of them then asked me what I would recommend for a "really good trip". That's when I really thought, what a pair of plonkers. So I asked them outright if they were undercover coppers. They nearly jumped out of their skins but denied it, naturally. I didn't give up, though. I started telling them how many coppers had tried to trick me and how a lawyer mate of mine said that was entrapment and they really should be careful not to do it because it would bounce back on them in a court of law.

'You should have seen the looks on their faces. They didn't know what to do but they were stuck there in the shop, so they had to keep up the pretence. They tried to make conversation with me about "smoke" but I blocked that one out by saying I didn't smoke. Then they picked up one of our sex stimulant products and asked really awkwardly if it was good for a hard-on.

'By that time I could hardly keep a straight face so I said as far as I was concerned the stuff was for polishing wooden tables (which it was) and my granny loved it and I was sure it was nothing to do with giving her a hard-on. At that moment one of them finally clicked that I had completely sussed them out and they turned on their heels and hotfooted it out of the store.'

But there is a much more serious side to running a legalhigh business on the high street. Ben explained: 'I get a lot of nasty looks from the older folk who walk past this place every day. They see us as the evil-high street drug dealers and no doubt they've read in the papers about some of the deaths associated to legal highs.

'But I have to tell you here and now that in my experience it's not the substances which kill anyone, it's the way they are handled by the customers. Let me explain: you should never take more than a minimum quantity. If it doesn't kick in, give it time. A lot of these products are slow burners. They can take as long as an hour to work and a lot of kids think they are like booze and will have an effect immediately.'

Ben continued: 'I know I'm not supposed to do this, but when we get very young teenagers in here I try to advise them in a roundabout way. If they look vulnerable and naive then I even sometimes advise them to avoid certain products they want to buy. I guess that coming from someone like me, they really do take notice because it's not exactly in my interests to put people off spending their money, is it?

'So you see, I am trying to be responsible to a certain degree. There is no point in taking stuff at an incredibly young age and having a bad experience, is there? Better to recommend something gentle to start with to give them a chance to work out for themselves if they can even handle drugs. I've lost count of the number of kids who've come back here a few days after buying a certain product and complaining that it was either too strong or too weak.'

In his own confused way, Ben knows that with his experience, his opinion is very valid to many teenagers. 'I've tried most of the products on display here myself and I know which ones work the best. I've never had a bad experience with them and me and my girlfriend like to experiment with stuff most weekends. I like to think it's research in a sense and that in many ways I'm helping the kids who come into this shop by being able to steer them clear of certain products I think don't suit their temperaments or character.'

Ben said he enjoyed his job immensely and hoped to do it for many years to come. 'I enjoy it because I'm an open sort of character and I like all the interaction with people.

LEGAL HIGHS

I get a real kick out of it when I bump into a customer in the street or a local pub and they tell me they had a great time on a certain product. I always say "I can't possibly comment" and then wink at them. It sort of sums up the situation in this business.'

CHAPTER 32

FRANKIE

Frankie works in a head shop in the Home Counties. He admitted that such businesses constantly live in fear that their products will be banned overnight but he still believes that herbal highs have a bright future.

Until recently Frankie also sold his legal-high products at a select number of music festivals across the south and west of England. 'They were the last bastion in a sense,' he told me. 'But we've been less and less involved with festivals over the last couple of years because they don't want us around any more. We'd like to set up a stall and soak up the passing trade. After all, that is where most of our core customers are in one place. It makes complete business sense.'

Frankie continued: 'The head-shop business didn't happen overnight. It's taken nearly ten years for them to properly take off. Now we get all types of people in here looking for legal highs. The most interesting thing about it, though, is that the Internet does not take any business from us. You see, that's a different sort of customer – the type who clinically orders it up before he even knows when he might be actually using the stuff.'

Frankie claimed that the music festival circuit had become much more tightly controlled in recent years. He explained: 'The councils and stuff are cracking down on us much more than before. Even the guys running the festivals have become more cautious and they've basically turned their backs on us. I think a lot of them are running scared in case anyone gets sick taking legal highs while they're on their premises.

'It's a real shame but we are paying the price for a lot of paranoia when it comes to legal highs,' Frankie went on. 'The festivals are being warned by authorities that they could be shut down if they allow legal highs to be sold on the premises. A few years back no one cared about this sort of thing. I guess it's tough if you're organizing a festival and you know that you won't get a licence next year if you in any way defy the law-makers. Seems ironic when you consider that festivals are supposed to be about freedom of expression.'

Nevertheless, Frankie realizes that festivals are not the be-all and end-all for the legal-high market: 'The legal-high trade is evolving every week. We've learned to adapt the business to whatever is happening in the world.' He blames a lot of what he calls 'the paranoia' on newspaper and TV reports about legal-high deaths. 'I'm sick of reading the headlines about legal highs killing people,' he declared. 'It's just not that simple. Sure, some people mix their drugs and take vast amounts of alcohol and that can combine to have a bad effect. But that is up to their personal choices. I tell people not to mix legal highs with other drugs or alcohol because it's obviously risky. Listen, hundreds of people die in accidents on the motorways but that doesn't stop others from driving on them, does it?'

Frankie also blamed the 'gentrification' of the drugs scene for many of the blanket bans on legal highs. 'Everyone wants to try them now which is great in one way but it's unfortunately brought legal highs to the attention of people who simply want them banned. They are now branding people who sell legal highs as criminals but how can that be? We are now part of the fabric of life in the UK. People who want legal highs go shopping and end up here. What's so wrong with that? At least I can give them the benefit of my experiences.'

Frankie still looks back nostalgically at the days when he would attend music festivals and openly smoke cannabis without being given a second glance. 'I'd like to think that one day all the legal highs will be acceptable at festivals again. I want people sitting round campfires playing the guitar and chilling out with a Spice reefer in their hand.

'You mark my words,' he predicted, 'it will happen one day. Just give it time. Who wants a world where everything is so safe that no one takes any risks any more?'

Frankie continued: 'We feel a bit betrayed by the law

because all we're doing is trying to run a legit business. We can't be held responsible for the future and that's what it feels like at the moment. When we started selling legal highs five or six years ago, everything seemed more relaxed, a bit more liberal. But even during that time the business has got bogged down in a morass of rules and regulations. It's as if the health and safety lot can't bear the idea of anyone having unsupervised fun. I reckon that in their ideal world, you'd have to fill in a form before you were allowed anywhere near anything that might get you high.'

Frankie was at pains to explain the lengths that he and his partners in the head-shop business went to test every single one of their products before they reached the marketplace. 'We're not idiots, we know that if we want people to trust us, we've got to sell them good stuff. And if we don't want the Old Bill breathing down our necks, it probably doesn't pay to have customers dying on us. So we get everything chemically tested – and we wouldn't sell anything that we wouldn't take ourselves.'

Frankie added: 'I'm sick of being treated like some kind of criminal out forcing drugs into the hands of teenagers. I'm a responsible adult who is trying his hardest to make a living out of something I have a personal interest in. I don't want people to die taking my products – but are supermarkets treated like killers for selling bars of chocolate that eventually kill off morbidly obese people?'

CHAPTER 33

KEN – HEAD-SHOP COP

I'm outside a head shop in a quiet town in the heart of Middle England that advertises synthetic marijuana and just about every other type of legal high available on the market. Schoolchildren and unemployed youths pour in and out of the store every day and local parents express fears about the substances on offer.

Detective Constable 'Ken' from the local police station sits in an unmarked car casing the shop on an overcast afternoon. He believes they're selling a vast range of potentially deadly legal highs around the clock. Any day now he'll raid the place.

Ken admitted it doesn't really matter if he charges in with search warrants and drags the owner out in cuffs, the shop will be back in business in no time. He knows such stores have spread like wildfire across the UK in recent years. In conversations with Ken, it became clear that there was little

265

he and his fellow officers could do in the long term to prevent these businesses from operating. 'Sure, I'm on their case constantly,' Ken asserted. 'It makes them more careful and if there is any suggestion that they're selling anything to people under the age of eighteen then we can come down on them like a ton of bricks.

'The head-shop owners and staff know they have to be very careful and we keep reminding them by being outside watching. I know it's not the same as actually arresting them outright for drug dealing but at least it shows we care. They know that they can get away with selling anything that's not covered by the anti-drug laws. But I'm on the lookout primarily to ensure that they do not actually recommend any of these substances which, after all, are not supposed to be for human consumption.'

Ken reckoned that most head shops were owned by wealthy businessmen who used staff to encourage the sale of high quantities of certain products before they were banned by law. 'It makes sense, doesn't it? If you've got stacks of one product and you know perfectly well that it's going to be banned very soon then you try your hardest to make sure they fly off the shelves. Then they try for a new formula that's not covered by the law until the same thing happens all over again.'

Ken explained that when a head shop was recently 'busted' for encouraging the sale of certain substances, the most the police could do was get a court order to close the store for a few days on suspicion of selling illegal substances.

'But, quite frankly, often it's not worth the trouble,' he pointed out. 'It's frustrating for the police because we know those substances are just as dangerous as illegal drugs.

'I've got two young children and I would hate it if a head shop opened for business round the corner from where I live. No wonder a lot of parents are constantly contacting us to say they want these businesses shut down. It's frustrating because I feel for all these parents.'

Ken added: 'We believe that a lot of these head shops encourage the kids who walk in to buy certain substances but proving that is another matter.'

Recently, Ken raided a head shop in another part of town and found to his horror that the owner was manufacturing his own brands of legal highs in the 'back office'. Ken explained: 'Obviously they were all dressed up as plant food not fit for human consumption but the packaging was very sloppy and I'm certain this was all being home produced in the office behind the counter. It was filthy dirty and the equipment consisted of a cooker, a few saucepans and some knives.'

Ken suspects that some head-shop owners have learned how to make the compounds for their especially popular synthetic weed by ordering the main substances directly from abroad, and then adding them to herbs and spices that can be bought in any supermarket.

Three weeks before I interviewed Ken, he raided a back-street legal-high factory in the countryside near the town where he works. 'Three Eastern Europeans were living in this barn attached to a farm and inside we found equipment and substances, which indicated they were manufacturing legal highs on the premises. In the end none of the substances were illegal themselves and when we spoke to the farmer who was renting them the barn he claimed he had no idea what they'd been up to.'

Ken said that the head-shop phenomenon was 'likely to grow and grow'. He explained: 'The overheads are very low. It costs next to nothing to open up a shop in a deprived, rundown high street where rents are low. And this is a growth industry. More people will go into a high-street head shop on a busy Saturday afternoon than most of the other struggling businesses around it.'

Ken's latest target is daubed in hand-painted graffiti of marijuana leafs and mushrooms with teenage stoner banners like 'Amsterdam', 'skunk' and 'feel' as well as the words 'incense store: not for human consumption' written on the walls.

Ken explained what you can expect to find in shops like this: 'The typical head shop is not an impressive place by any means. It usually consists of a counter and a load of sloppy-looking displays containing various of the softer legal highs that are on sale all over the UK, everywhere from petrol stations to mobile-phone repair shops. But my biggest concern is what substances the head-shop staff are offering the youngsters when they ask for something stronger.

'One of my colleagues in another nearby town managed

to get a head shop closed down because they had evidence that certain illegal substances were being offered under the counter to youngsters. Well, within three days, the same head-shop owner had walked into a nearby corner shop newsagent and persuaded the owner to sell all his old legal-high stock over the counter. It's incredible how these products have been accepted by small businesses who believe that because they are legal they are not a risk to anyone's health.'

Ken went on: 'I've even heard that a lot of kids smoke synthetic cannabis because they know that it is undetectable in the DIY drug kits which a lot of parents now use to test if their children are on drugs. But I believe these substances can often be more dangerous than their illegal counterparts.'

He suspects that a lot of the head-shop owners are former hash dealers 'who've decided to turn over a new leaf'. 'Some of these characters were criminals who thought they'd go straight by flogging legal highs, many of which are just as deadly to consume.'

Ken says he is deeply frustrated at the police's inability to stop a drug trade that is out in the open and anything but harmless.

'See this head shop right there?' he said, pointing out of his car window at the store he was watching. 'It's a shithole. Probably cost the owner a few hundred quid to set up but I know that just a few months after being opened, he was able to buy himself a brand new Mercedes. These people are no better than the old-fashioned drug dealers in my book.'

Ken added: 'My own theory is that only people power can get these places shut down. Dozens and dozens of parents in this area want these head shops shut down and in the end the politicians will wake up to the menace that they represent and come up with some law or other which will enable the police to close them all permanently.'

Ken also disclosed that other high-street traders were starting to openly sell legal highs across the UK. 'These shops usually sell something that kids are interested in like phones or DVDs,' explained Ken.

Phil the Phone Man is a classic example . . .

CHAPTER 34

PHIL THE PHONE MAN

Outlets ranging from petrol stations to newsagents stock many of the more commercial, so-called 'softer' legal highs openly on their display shelves these days. It's believed that some traders deliberately open youth-orientated businesses knowing full well that their core customers will be interested in purchasing legal highs as well as the main product on sale.

Take Phil the Phone Man. He runs his own mobile-phone repair shop in a town in the Midlands with notoriously high unemployment but openly admitted that he makes more cash from the sale of legal highs available in his shop. 'I hate illegal drugs,' he exclaimed. 'I think they're the scourge of this nation but these things . . .' He pointed to the display of brightly coloured products to the left of his counter. '. . . They are harmless as far as I am concerned and the suppliers assure me they're completely legal. I don't see why I should not be selling them, do you?'

Phil has been repairing mobile phones for ten years but claimed that his business was on its last legs until a salesman walked into his store one day and offered him a way out of his financial problems. 'This guy was just like any other salesman but his products didn't seem to have any connection to my business. I couldn't understand why he was bothering to come in here in the first place. He was carrying a load of sample packets in a briefcase and when I first looked at them, I thought they were all sweets and stuff like that and told him he'd come to the wrong place.

'They had strange names like Bazooka and Feline and I was pretty confused at first. Then he sat down and explained that these were what they called legal highs and that the demand for them was phenomenal and that my business would double its turnover if I stocked them prominently.

'I was sceptical at first. I couldn't see how these funny-looking things could attract anyone into my shop but this guy was very convincing, so I agreed to take an initial order and see how they went. Well, they sold like hotdogs. I was astounded. It only then dawned on me that I'd been targeted by that salesman because of the mainly young customers I get in my phone shop.

'Teenagers can't afford new phones, so they often ask me to repair them. A lot of them spend hours looking at the new models I have in a display cabinet without having enough money to purchase them. And that's when they see that I'm also selling legal highs. The other great advantage I have is that the kids who come in here often wait while I try to fix their phones on the spot. That gives them loads of time to spot the legal highs on the counter.'

Phil said he was convinced that all the products he sold would have been carefully tested, although he was astounded when I pointed out that at least three of the products were mainly used as sex stimulants and that one product, GHB, had been linked to numerous deaths in recent years yet remained unbanned by UK authorities.

'I'm sorry to hear that people have died taking the stuff but I've been assured by the suppliers that these products have been properly licensed. I mean, you can tell from the packaging because it is very professional. A lot of kids come in here regularly just to buy these products from me.

'I asked one group of kids why they didn't just order the stuff off the Internet and they said they didn't want the packages turning up at their homes because their parents might make a fuss. They also said they trusted the products more if they could handle the packs before they bought them, which was fair enough.'

Phil admitted that demand for his legal-high products was so high that he believed 'at least half the customers who now walk into my shop are only coming to buy them.' He added: 'Getting phones fixed is now playing second fiddle to the legal highs. I can't complain because it's all income for me. I must admit it was clever the way that salesman and his bosses at the wholesalers worked out that a business like mine would be so good for their products.'

The wholesalers who supply Phil with all his legal highs refused to discuss their sourcing when I contacted them. But Phil said he'd talked at length with them about the background to their business and what he was told was intriguing. 'Oh, the salesman told me that virtually all the products were made in China but that they had been given a proper export licence to come into the UK and that was stated clearly on the packaging. What amazed me was that some of these products, especially what you say are sex stimulants, can be so openly sold. I didn't need a special licence and I've never once been visited by any standards inspectors or people like that.'

Compare that to the head shops, many of whom claim they're constantly harassed by their local police who suspect them of breaking the law by recommending products labelled with the phrase 'Unfit for Human Consumption'.

'I don't want to knock anyone because the legal-high business has been good to me but I don't really get any of this. It seems very inconsistent,' said Phil. 'If I went out today and started a head shop then they'd all come down on me like a ton of bricks. But because I run a phone shop that sells legal highs I seem to slip below the radar. Now that is great news for me but it does make me wonder what is legal and what isn't legal. It's bloody confusing.'

Meanwhile Phil's business goes from strength to strength.

'I believe my products are at the safer end of the market, which is very different from some of the heavier things on offer on the Internet. But the kids seem to be lapping them up and as far as I can see they're not doing them any harm, so what's the problem?

'That salesman came in here the other day with some replacement products which he insisted were needed because one of the substances I stocked had been banned. It was no big deal, he simply swapped them at no charge to me, so I have no complaints and if the system works like that then surely it's fine, isn't it? The last thing I want is somebody dying after taking something they bought in my shop.'

PART SEVEN

THE FUTURE

While new harmful substances have been emerging with unfailing regularity on the drug scene, the international drug control system is floundering, for the first time, under the speed and creativity of the phenomenon.

United Nations' *World Drug Report*

CHAPTER 35

LEGAL-HIGH HEROIN

Besides dozens of new products manufactured round the clock to replicate the effects of cocaine, cannabis and Ecstasy, it is feared that brand-new, much more deadly designer drugs – with a similar effect to heroin – will almost certainly lead to a surge in legal high-related deaths.

One such psychoactive is called AH-7921 and it's already cost at least one life in the UK. Father-of-one Jason Nock, forty-one, died in August 2013 after accidentally overdosing on the legal morphine-like drug he had purchased online for £25 to help him sleep. The computer technician, from Cradley Heath, West Midlands, accidentally took enough of the unregulated substance, more commonly known as Doxylam, to kill himself five times over, and never woke up.

'If this stuff gets a grip on the young, it could turn into a drug epidemic because it is highly addictive,' claimed one expert. 'There are sites out there on the Internet offering it and making it clear that it is comparable to heroin. A lot of curious youngsters may well fall into the trap of buying it.'

Meanwhile other substances are emerging, many of which come from very different sources to the traditional legal highs. In Washington State, most legal highs were outlawed in 2010. However, a product called Kratom has recently become widely available and can be purchased across the counter of many stores. Kratom has been used in Asian countries for many years. But US law enforcement agencies and numerous members of the medical profession have labeled Kratom a lethal drug that is not only highly addictive but also deadly if used to excess.

Kratom itself comes in a tree leaf form and is closely aligned to the coffee tree. It is then ground down into a powder and mixed with water. But America's Drug Enforcement Agency insists it has no legitimate medical purpose. In the UK, Kratom has been dubbed 'herbal speedball' by users.

Recently US TV exposed Kratom's emergence in Washington when the Fox 13 channel interviewed a user called Lisa. She bought her Kratom from a Capitol Hill smoke shop, which was similar to the head shops that exist in the UK. She claimed it helped control her anxiety and depression. 'I'm on every pharmaceutical drug known to man; that's not working for me,' Lisa said. 'When I discovered this, it's taken almost all of my symptoms away.'

Users of Kratom openly admit that few people even know of its existence. But googling the word provides ample evidence that it is easily available on the Internet. That helped highlight it to authorities in the US and UK. In Washington State alone, authorities say that at least half a dozen people call in each year fearing they've overdosed on Kratom.

'I think it's prone to abuse and I think if you take too much, it can be very harmful,' toxicologist Thomas Martin told the Fox 13 investigation into the use of Kratom.

The DEA insists Kratom is not only addictive, but it's also led directly to extremely serious medical conditions. The agency cites several cases of Kratom psychosis in Thailand in which addicts' symptoms included hallucinations, delusions and confusion.

Users claim that low doses of Kratom are relatively harmless and that it works like a stimulant – but at higher doses it acts like a sedative. 'It has both opioid-like properties and stimulant-like properties,' Thomas Martin told Fox 13. 'Some people believe you can use it to help withdrawal from opioid addiction more safely.'

Despite the health fears surrounding Kratom, it has yet to be classified as a controlled substance in the same ways that other so-called 'innocent' products such as bath salts have been.

Meanwhile Lisa is hopeful Kratom will continue to be readily available. 'Let's hope it keeps going and that they don't do anything about it because it's saving my life right now,' she said.

The benefits of banning legal highs completely far outweigh those of keeping the status quo and simply tightening regulations, say many of the experts I've interviewed for this book.

Admittedly, the definition of legal highs and the amorphous nature of their chemical composition makes this extremely hard to achieve. But law enforcement agencies across the Western World are convinced that clever lawmakers could ensure the process of proving beyond all doubt that substances being brought into the country were legal would be so costly for anyone wanting to import these products, that it could eventually kill off the legal-high phenomenon. This would include the importation of any substances used to create home-produced legal highs as well.

In New Zealand – where legal highs took off in much the same way they did in Guernsey but on a much larger scale – tests were carried out on humans, which confirmed all the health professionals' worst fears about their deadly potential. Hospital accident and emergency statistics also provide overwhelming evidence that all legal highs can be lethal. Making legal-high traders prove their products are harmless sounds like the answer but defining what is harmless may prove virtually impossible.

Many experts believe that if this breed of synthetic narcotics were to be completely banned, then those who were dependent on them will simply find something else to help them get high. That said, the majority of users are said to be broadly similar to cannabis smokers in terms of their attitude towards other drugs. Research shows that a large number of them are often not interested in cocaine and heroin because they consider them to be much more dangerous and addictive – although the legal highs aimed at that 'market' will no doubt contradict this in the long term.

So an outright ban might well push large numbers of legal-high users towards using illicit drugs, which would be great news for narco-gangs from Colombia to Morocco. However, having said that, it used to be thought that these kinds of designer drugs would lose their popularity if they were banned – the consensus being that in the event of prohibition users would go back to the old-style illegal narcotics for their highs. But this has already been repeatedly contradicted by the examples highlighted in this book.

In the US, the country's all-powerful Drug Enforcement Agency admitted in 2013 that it 'doesn't have the tools to keep up with the rapidly expanding market for legal highs'.

I visited the DEA in Florida in the summer of 2013 and it was clear that the US is bracing itself because of the clear evidence that international criminal gangs were expanding even further into the burgeoning legal-high market.

My DEA contact explained: 'This is a nightmare for all law enforcement agencies. How can governments including us here in the US feasibly monitor the marketplace for so-called legal highs? Folks out there just don't seem to realize that banning a new drug is a complicated process and many countries simply don't bother, so most of these substances remain available on the Internet. It's no wonder that drug gangs are focusing in on this illegal market. They've spotted a huge gap in the market and they are taking full advantage of it.'

The DEA are well aware that so-called 'traditional drugs' are going out of fashion. 'They're much harder to transport. It's a no brainer for any criminal looking for a new, lucrative marketplace. Sure, heroin and coke still cause havoc but legal highs are sweeping across the drug world, and one thing's for sure, they've totally changed the game.'

Meanwhile, US law enforcement agencies continue to tactfully urge other nations to follow their lead by bringing in even swifter legislation to ensure the banning of any new drugs. In the US, a system called scheduling of analogues ensures that drugs similar in effect or chemical make-up to existing illegal drugs can be speedily banned. However, the ban by American lawmakers on broad classes or base molecules rather than specific chemical compounds comes with additional problems as chemists simply search wider for alternatives that achieve a similar high and encounter greater unknowns (and therefore risks) as a consequence. This tactic is also controversial because many consumers only learn that substances are in fact outlawed when a case reaches the courtroom, with law enforcement often penalizing the users rather than preventing the drugs entering the country at source. The US's efforts to crack down on legal highs in many ways mirrors its efforts to outlaw terrorism. They are convinced that more cooperation between nations and special efforts to track down, then identify, new substances and finally cut off the distribution network are the only ways to stop the influx of legal highs turning into a veritable tidal wave.

Back in June 2012, the DEA launched the largest-ever operation to break up a global synthetic-drugs ring. Project Synergy seized thousands of pounds of illicit drugs and saw the arrest of 225 people in five countries. The same month, members of the G8 group of nations signed an agreement to share information and intelligence regarding legal highs. In the end, however, Project Synergy proved to be nothing more than a slap on the wrist for potential dealers by warning them they risked arrest if involved. Ongoing smuggling networks were barely affected.

But the cooperative approach being pioneered by the US authorities is by no means the only way for countries to deal with the designer drug phenomenon. And some nations have taken radically different approaches. Legal highs have taken off in New Zealand faster than anywhere else in the world. Conventional hard drugs have always been scarce in this country, because traffickers have little interest in serving four million people far out in the South Pacific. Kiwis therefore make their own synthetic drugs, which they take in greater quantity than virtually anyone else. Some years ago the NZ government shut down more crystal-meth labs there than anywhere except America and Ukraine.

As a result of that crackdown there was a huge opening for legal highs in New Zealand. Initially many of this country's young turned to benzylpiperazine, which a third of young New Zealanders eventually tried. When that was banned in 2008, dealers found plenty of other chemicals to peddle. Today the most popular highs are synthetic cannabinoids, which are renowned for packing a harder punch than ordinary cannabis.

In New Zealand in July 2013, legislators adopted a new tack by passing a law which offered drug designers the chance to get official approval for their products. If they could persuade a panel called the 'Psychoactive Substances Regulatory Authority' that their pills and powders were low risk, they'd be licensed to market them, whether or not they get people high.

These substances would have to even undergo clinical trials, which the government expected to take around eighteen months – much less than for medicines, because the drugs would be tested only for toxicity, not for efficacy. Drugs that were already banned internationally, such as cocaine and cannabis, would be ineligible. Only licensed shops could sell the drugs, without advertising and not to children. But so far NZ's new scheme has not been fully implemented.

By contrast, in Eastern Europe authorities are more inclined to pursue a more aggressive course of action. The former Soviet republic of Belarus is said to be fighting a losing battle with consumption of legal highs, many of which have been outlawed in the country but continue to be taken in huge quantities.

One anti-drug campaigner, Andrei Dzmitryeu, claimed the problem was so overwhelming that Belarus should seriously consider the death penalty for anyone caught dealing in drugs, including substances classified as legal highs in other countries. He said: 'We propose to introduce a more severe punishment for drug trafficking of up to ten to fifteen years in a high-security prison and even the death penalty in some special cases.'

Dzmitryeu reckoned drugs should be completely outlawed and that any talks about legalization are 'assistance to those who want the Belarusian people to disappear'.

During the first three months of 2014, seven young people died in the capital of Minsk after eating blotting paper that contained a synthetic drug. Numerous teenagers were said to have been seriously poisoned and ended up in hospital in various cities across the country during the same period.

When the Belarus government attempted to ban the synthetic cannabis legal high called Spice they found it impossible to implement because of the drug's easy access via the Internet. According to Belarusian law enforcement, China, Myanmar, Thailand and Indonesia produce around 800 tonnes of the synthetic drug annually. The substance reaches Belarus either in ready-to-smoke blends, in powder form, on blotting paper or as a pure substance that dealers can prepare for usage domestically.

In Belarus, the apparent success of Spice can be attributed to its legal status there. And throughout the country, demand for legal highs has shot up over the past two years. One dealer I spoke to confirmed that easy access to substances on the World Wide Web had undoubtedly provided what some have called a 'drugs epidemic'. Recently, the Belarus police have been given sweeping new powers to shut down many of the legal-high websites. But one dealer I spoke to said that that had pushed his business 'onto the streets'. He explained: 'It's no big deal. I just sell it direct to all the people I used to supply from the Internet.' But this dealer and others I spoke to were angry that Belarus officials had even been publicly calling for the death penalty for anyone caught selling legal highs. 'Listen,' said the dealer. 'People here are bored out of their brains. There is nothing to do except take stuff to try and escape the mundane level of life here. Legal highs provide that high. I am simply feeding a demand. I have a connection with the kids here and they trust me to provide them with stuff that makes their lives more bearable. What is so wrong about that?'

Britain's own attempts to police its legal-high market have been perhaps closer to those of the US than to the two poles represented by New Zealand and Belarus.

One UK drug enforcement spokesman told the *Guardian* newspaper: 'One of the efforts we're pioneering in the UK and other partners in the G8 is encouraging the World Health Organisation to dedicate increased resources to identifying and scheduling of new psychoactive substances [and] create a more robust regime.' He said there would also be an emphasis on demand reduction and treatment, as well as preventing the sale and use of such drugs, and that help would be made available to countries lacking expertise in these areas. But so far none of these measures have actually been sanctioned and these proposals seem unlikely to be activated in the near future.

Despite several attempts to impose blanket curbs, world-wide law enforcement agencies continue to 'flounder', says the UN's Office on Drugs and Crime. Nevertheless, the UN is reluctant to heap blame on China or any of the other countries that provide many of the substances used to manufacture legal highs. 'The demand is here and we have to take responsibility for that,' a UN spokesman told the *Guardian*. 'We need to address this problem by getting the users to stop using. That should be our priority.'

While the UK authorities have begun to make increasingly robust efforts to combat what they consider to be a growing scourge, their energy occasionally has proved to be somewhat misdirected. In 2014, a British father-of-two was jailed for selling thousands of pounds' worth of 'legal high' drugs, which then became illegal. The man had previously run his own business selling the drugs online and he genuinely did not believe he was breaking the law. As one London police detective said after the case: 'These sort of convictions send out a message to any law-abiding people planning to set up a legal-high business but we need to address the core problem of the criminals who are running so many of the country's legal-high supply routes.'

Back in December 2010, the UK government suggested that drug dealers who sold deadly psychotropics could potentially face up to fourteen years in jail, even before the substances they were selling had been permanently banned. But that 'get tough' policy proved hard to implement and there are still numerous examples of dealers of legal highs being let off with cautions by overworked and under-resourced police forces.

In fact, half the time coppers find that their job is less policing, more fact-finding. British nightclubs regularly search patrons upon entry and place any suspicious substances in so-called 'amnesty bins' that are regularly emptied by police. When they see anything potentially new, police often forward the substance to a toxicologist who keeps a vast database of new drugs. These experts specialize in identifying new substances, and have witnessed an explosion in the numbers of legal-high users in recent years.

Police also hear about new drugs on the market from hospital A&E departments. In the summer of 2014, a hospital in north-west England phoned local police after six people in a single week reported taking the legal high 'Ivory Wave'. They'd come to the hospital appearing 'paranoid and extremely agitated', with extremely fast heart rates. It took four members of staff to restrain one young woman, who was eventually sent to a mental institution, where she remained for months of treatment. Another victim of this substance was a man of twenty-four whose body was found in the sea off the Isle of Wight in the summer of 2010 after he'd apparently fallen from a 300ft cliff. A witness said the man appeared to be pretending he could fly.

James Brokenshire, the then minister for crime reduction

at the UK's Home Office, said police were encouraging hospitals to keep them informed about legal-high threats. Law enforcement agencies also monitor websites for evidence of new drugs and, as mentioned previously in this book, they have stepped up visits to head shops to keep track of what's being sold and to carefully keep an eye on what products are stocked on the shelves of such premises.

But the UK's Association of Chief Police Officers admitted they are still struggling to cope with the new strands of legal highs created in pharmacies abroad and sold via the Internet. The police said they were ill-equipped to identify and ban particular substances, especially when another version is then quickly released onto the marketplace, either online or via dealers.

A sign of the difficulty of creating coherent policy supported at every level from the top down came in 2014. The UK's top police officers pledged they'd treat anyone found with one of these substances leniently, meaning that the holder could be cautioned instead of having to go to court. In the eyes of the British police, dealers are their priority and arresting users would do nothing except push the legal-high business further underground. But this announcement was seen as an embarrassment for the UK government, who were in the middle of preparing new powers to deal with the explosion in legal-high drug use.

Instead of using overworked police, there have been suggestions the government should use existing consumer protection legislation to tackle legal highs. The police continue to demand that owners of shops selling legal highs should be made liable for any subsequent harm to the user from a legal high purchased on their premises.

The British police have instituted an Early Warning System on New Psychoactive Substances. This includes monitoring the Internet for the emergence of new products and keeping close tabs on any criminal cases involving the importation or production of legal highs. Police have also pledged to work closely with the European Monitoring Centre for Drugs and Drug Action – a group comprising scientists, health professions and law enforcement agencies. This partnership helps them keep up to date with legislation and allows them to carry out the monitoring of drugs use. But many believe it is a case of too little, too late.

On a local level, UK police, trading standards and public health officials have recently increased the pressure on vendors of legal highs by raiding high-street stores, car boot sales, markets and arresting street dealers, as well as cracking down on legal-high websites.

In Lincolnshire in December 2013, police launched Operation Burdock to tackle a dramatic increase in the number of people being taken ill after using legal highs in the county. Chief Inspector Pat Coates, who led the operation, said at the time: 'I've seen so many people in our custody suites, whose behaviour has been down to what they've taken. It's often erratic and very aggressive, confrontational and violent. I've seen a fifteen-year-old go to intensive care and thankfully then make a full recovery. Schools come to us constantly and say pupils are becoming ill and they've no idea what they've ingested.'

Lincolnshire County Council recently launched a campaign aimed at educating people who believed that legal highs were harmless. 'Just because you can buy them in a shop doesn't mean you should drink or eat it,' said a spokesman for the council. 'None of these substances have been in any way tested. You wouldn't drink bathroom cleaner just because it came from a shop. Some people have absolutely no idea what they're putting into their bodies. And the problem with our clinicians dealing with poisoning is they don't know what they're dealing with because patients can't tell them.'

In the West of England, it's a similar story. Detective Constable Jon Manning, Plymouth police's drug liaison officer, said: 'In recent years, we've seen a significant rise in the number of New Psychoactive Substances which has rapidly changed the nature of the global drugs marketplace. Organized criminals have exploited the existing drugs market with these substances. We have also seen head shops appearing on our high streets which on "face value" appear to comply with existing legislation, making this a complex multi-agency issue to resolve.'

The UK's then crime prevention minister Norman Baker admitted: 'The fact is there is a problem that hasn't yet been dealt with satisfactorily, both in this country and elsewhere. And that's a challenge, which we collectively face. In particular I'm concerned by the shocking emergence of new substances designed to have similar effects to heroin and synthetic opiates.

'We have a changing landscape in the drug world,' he continued. 'The drugs which we have traditionally wrestled with, which have been there for decades if not longer, are now being added to by these new psychoactive substances. It presents a challenge because if they are perceived to be legal and they suddenly arrive in our country before they have obviously been banned, then young people in particular can conclude that they are safe when they are nothing of the kind.' He added that the government had decades of history and analysis about the effects of cocaine and heroin, which has helped them to come up with a policy. But no such knowledge existed about some legal highs.

Baker said the Advisory Council on the Misuse of Drugs, which advises the government on whether a drug should be banned or reclassified, would continue to closely monitor developments. He also appointed experts in toxicology, policing, education, health and prevention onto the review panel into legal highs in a bid to get a proper handle on the subject. He concluded by emphasizing that certain legal highs were 'more dangerous' than heroin or cocaine. 'People think they are safe and legal when they may not be,' he pointed out. 'So I have initiated a review of so-called legal highs, which are a particular problem at the moment and becoming more serious than some of the traditional drugs in many ways.'

Yet the minister admitted that he and his UK colleagues

were refusing to sign up to European legislation for tackling the legal highs because the proposal would restrict Britain's ability to control the drugs. Mr Baker said that the government disputed European Union evidence, which estimated that 20 per cent of legal highs had a 'legitimate use'.

In London, Scotland Yard's Operation Titan was set up in 2013 to monitor developments in the legal-high market and coordinate activity across the UK in order to raise awareness of the threat from such substances. The UK's National Crime Agency (NCA), Border Force, Her Majesty's Prisons and Trading Standards all took part in a week of enforcement on new 'legal highs' from 25 November to 1 December 2013. Officers from Operation Titan visited head shops and arrested more than forty people as well as seizing cash, illegal drugs and a firearm in police raids deliberately carried out to disrupt the market in new psychoactive substances.

Titan head Detective Chief Superintendent Dermott Horrigan said: 'Across the country, we have had some significant arrests and recoveries sending a clear message to the suppliers of these dangerous drugs that the police and other agencies are coming for you. We will now be analysing the information and intelligence we've gathered over the week so we can continue to tackle this serious threat to our communities.'

UK law enforcement swoops on so-called head shops were specifically aimed to show clearly that 'legal highs' could not be assumed to be safe or legal. In Kent, police took away multiple 'numbers of legal highs' for analysis. One head shop handed over nine kilograms for testing as they had no proof of the origin or content of the products on their shelves. Other head shops in Avon and Somerset removed all their products following the police raids.

The UK's National Policing Lead for New Psychoactive Substances, Commander Simon Bray said: 'Those supplying NPS very often have no idea what they are selling and don't care about the health and safety of those buying the products. Many of the products advertised as "legal highs" contain controlled drugs and, in some cases, their production and supply is linked to organized crime groups trading in illegal drugs, firearms and weapons. These results show the action that police and partners can take to restrict the availability of these drugs on our streets and tackle the criminality involved in the industry.'

Another more 'Hearts and Minds' approach has been trialled in Bedfordshire. Here the police sent messages to known addicts and users as part of a national week of action in 2014 targeting those supplying and using such chemicals. Officers contacted all those people in their county who were known to have purchased these drugs online for personal use, with the aim of raising awareness and warning users of the dangers but also warning these users that possessing such substances is a criminal offence.

But the police showed a softer side by insisting on issuing a stark warning to all the legal-high users they interviewed. 'If you choose to take a drug, don't take a second pill because you think it isn't working. Some drugs take a lot longer than others to take effect and you can never be sure about what you have taken.'

In another part of the UK – Dorset – suspected users of legal highs were also sent letters by the local police in a bid to discourage people from taking them. As in Bedfordshire, officers wrote to people believed to have bought the drugs over the Internet and also visited a number of suspected suppliers. Further visits were planned. The operation was aimed at stemming the supply of the products and raising awareness of their potential dangers.

Only time will tell whether all of this activity by lawmakers and law-enforcers alike will have any impact on the ever-growing business of legal highs.

According to one report in *Time* magazine, in the summer of 2014, many unregistered substances such as 5-MAPB – designed as a legal replacement for the infamous Benzo Fury (or 6-APDB) – continued to be openly sold on the Internet. And there was apparently no problem with supply. A Cyprus-based website called drsynthetic.com was exposed by *Time* magazine offering 'stimulants, cannabinoids and hallucinogenic [chemicals]' from 'our laboratory in China' with up to '1 kilo per day per client of any kind of our products. We work fast and discreet.'

Meanwhile, horror stories of the terrible destruction legal highs can wreak continue to flood the British media. In the summer of 2014, the *Daily Mail* published a chilling photograph of the terrible damage that an addiction to a legal high had wrought on the features of a girl who, only a couple of years previously, had aspired to being an air hostess.

The *Mail* told how the woman had once been an attractive blonde with clear skin, good teeth and a desire to go places. But this all changed once she'd developed a taste for the legal high GBL. (GBL – or gamma butyrolactone – is used in some paint strippers, nail varnish removers and superglue solvents. Although it was officially outlawed by the UK government in December 2009, it is still possible to obtain online as a cheap industrial cleaner.) This soon developed into a chronic addiction which left her with severe liver damage and the unenviable record of having been on life support an unbelievable fifteen times in the course of the 1,000 times she had been hospitalized in just four years. The addiction changed her physical appearance almost completely. Her blonde locks turned an unappealing shade of mousy brown, her skin became a blotchy mess and she lost her teeth after a drug-induced fall.

She stopped taking the narcotic only after doctors warned her that, if she didn't, she was likely to die. 'Doctors told me that, if I did GBL or drank alcohol again, I would be dead. It was a real wake-up call. No one had ever told me I could die from it. I could not believe I had let it get this far.'

Having now finally got off GBL, the woman claimed she'd been clean for two years and was determined to get her life back on track. The recovering addict – whose eighteen-month-old daughter was taken away from her at the height of her drug abuse – also spoke of her hope that she would soon be reunited with her child once again. She told the *Daily Mail*: 'I'm ashamed to admit I loved GBL more than her,' she said. 'I will never forgive myself for letting drugs come between me and my daughter.'

Thanks to her chronic GBL addiction, the woman's life expectancy has been reduced by at least ten years – and she admitted she looked far older than other women in their twenties. Meanwhile, her liver operated at a level of just 11 per cent, meaning she would need a transplant in the future.

In June 2014, in another part of the UK, two junkies were photographed slumped on the floor of a public toilet after injecting themselves with a legal high. The two addicts had injected themselves just yards from a popular park full of adults and children at lunch time in the Somerset town of Taunton. The pair were thought to have bought the legal highs from a nearby shop before going into the toilet in broad daylight for a fix. When police arrived one of the men came round while it took around ten minutes to wake the other from his drug-fuelled daze. No arrests could be made because the men were not in possession of any illegal substances. Avon and Somerset police condemned their behaviour and said they feared it was only a matter of time before a child pricked themselves on one of their discarded needles.

In 2013, it was reported in *Time* magazine in the US that legal highs were directly linked to a mass hospitalization of guests at a house party in Blaine, Minnesota. The psycho-actives had arrived in an 'unnamed, unmarked package', according to one youth quoted in *Time*. The rest of what happened that night is horrific. Those who took the 2C-E – one of the myriad Ecstasy substitutes on the market – began sweating, shaking, rolling around on the floor and experiencing seizures and severe pain.

Ten people were eventually hospitalized, while one nineteen-year-old partygoer – father of a five-month-old baby – died after 'punching walls, breaking items, staring and having dilated pupils and yelling', according to one witness who spoke to *Time*. The youth who supplied the legal highs at the house party is currently serving a ten-year sentence for third-degree unintentional murder in a state correctional facility. He said: 'I feel horrible. I feel horrible for his family – I was close to his mum before – and I feel horrible for anyone who knew him. There's not a day that goes by when I don't think about him. Every day the first thing I do is look at his picture on my bulletin board in my room and say a prayer for his family.'

EPILOGUE

You can't just separate what's illegal and what's legal because on the street that really doesn't make much difference anyway.

Haydn Morris, CEO
of Surrey Addictions Advisory Service

'It's all a matter of the quantities you take,' a London legal-high 'chemist' called Joe said with a shrug of the shoulders when I asked him how the future would pan out when it came to legal highs. 'Consumers need to appreciate that legal highs are often a fuck sight stronger than most illegal drugs or more and more people will die. I encourage my customers to take very small amounts at all times.'

Yet despite dabbling as a legal-high dealer, Joe is convinced that legalizing all drugs and 'selling them in corner shops with proper packaging and instructions on the back would be best for everyone'. He added: 'It would not only earn governments around the world massive amounts of cash through taxation but it would also cut out many of the dangers we hear about every day.'

Joe went on: 'I specialize in turning legal highs into illegal highs by cooking the stuff up and then turning it into paste, then tablets or powder. But I'd be more than happy if all drugs were legalized.

'I'm not a hardened criminal. I just enjoy selling my produce to a small, select group of friends and acquaintances. The so-called real gangsters are thriving on the illegal status of all drugs. When they banned Meow Meow a few years ago it was like a dream come true for drug dealers because people came to them demanding it in even bigger quantities than what they bought when it was legal.

'You see, if a drug is banned it makes a lot of people think it must be half decent. Governments are creating new drug markets by outlawing stuff, not stamping out drug use. When are they going to get it?'

Joe added: 'The reality when it comes to legal highs is that they've only just taken off and the usage of such substances is going to sky-rocket over the next few years.'

Joe is a useful barometer of the situation because he's based in the heart of London, where more legal highs are consumed at clubs and parties every weekend than probably anywhere else on the globe.

'Where's it all going from here? That's the question I get asked over and over again,' said Joe. 'I predict that as more and more people take these drugs, the generational aspect of legal-high consumption will disappear. You'll get many people over the age of fifty taking them. And as everyone's wage packets continue to shrink, so will their spending power. Let me explain: an old boy who's taken coke for half his life on a recreational basis won't be able to afford a few grams on his pension. But if he comes across Meow Meow at £10 a gram on the Internet, he's going to hoover it up, literally!'

Joe, now forty-one, has been taking drugs since the age of twelve and both his parents had a heroin problem, so he is talking from experience. 'I'm a classic example. I was brought up in a heavy drug-use environment and I can't see myself ever stopping taking stuff myself. Mind you, I never touch alcohol. That wrecks people's lives a lot more than legal highs. I have a safe nine-to-five job as well as making a few bob cooking up my own versions of all sorts of these substances.

'I know who is out there and who is taking all these drugs and it's mindblowing. I know an oil billionaire, aged sixty, in Mayfair who buys ten grams of mephedrone every week. I sometimes make him my own special version of Salvia, which he says blows his mind so much that he only uses it occasionally. At the other end of the social scale are the twenty-somethings whom I deal with who're using legal highs mainly because they are cheaper than alcohol to consume. That sums it up, eh?'

Meanwhile, the legitimate legal-high experts seem completely lost in a sea of meaningless statistics and case studies.

One co-author of the UN's latest report on the legal-high epidemic told me: 'We try to make our reports accurate but we can't keep up with the amount of people turning to legal highs every week.

'It takes two years to produce and then publish a full report and by that time most of our information is out of date and relatively inaccurate. Legal highs in some form or other are here to stay.

'Governments can't keep up with the new ones coming on the market every month and, quite frankly, neither can we. The key, in my opinion, is for governments to stop treating them like all the, as it were, illegal drugs such as cannabis, cocaine, Ecstasy and heroin.

'The US's attempts to stamp out the cocaine market in the eighties failed miserably and so will any attempt at a similar plan regarding legal highs. Alcohol is a much bigger problem, healthwise, and yet that continues to be socially acceptable, so how on earth can anyone expect to stamp out legal-high usage?

'We all know that alcohol will never be outlawed, so we need to work out a way to nurture the legal-high industry and try to "convert" it into something legitimate with proper quality controls and some kind of rating system, so that people buying them actually know what they are getting.

'But unfortunately, this sort of move would be considered political suicide in most Western countries so we are left with no realistic reaction to the problem. This allows legal highs to gain popularity without ever being legitimately checked for quality. It's a very predictable scenario.'

So there you have it. As the worldwide marketplace for legal highs continues to increase exponentially, even the experts shrug their shoulders and accept that they are here to stay – and so, for the time being, are the hard-nosed criminals cashing in on a drug craze that many predict will never go away.

Joe summed it up perfectly: 'Politicians spend their lives trying to give the impression their job is to do things "for the people". Well, the people want legal highs by the bucketload so pledging to stamp them out is pretty stupid, isn't it? I reckon within the next twenty years legal highs will be taken by the majority of the population at some time or other which means demand will continue to increase and the fat-cat criminals will simply get fatter. Maybe then, and only then, governments will wake up and do something.'

APPENDIX

LETHAL LEGAL HIGHS

It's believed that there may be thousands of legal highs out there, so it's impossible to mention them all. However, the ten substances listed here are undoubtedly among the most dangerous and popular. Many have now been outlawed but carefully 'tweaked' versions of them are still easily available through dealers, on the Web and in head shops.

1. Spice
It's known as the nearest thing to smoking real marijuana but side-effects are far reaching and often disturbing.
2. 2M2B
(2-methyl-2-butanol) Real purpose is as a pharmaceutical or pigment solvent but in recent years it's appeared on many legal-high websites where it is marketed as a depressant and intoxicant, but it has never been properly tested on humans.

3. Bromo Dragonfly

Renowned as an extremely potent psychedelic, it has gained a devoted following among psychonauts. But it is considered one of the most dangerous legal highs of all time.

4. O-Desmethyltramadol

A member of the Tramadol 'family' of drugs, it's supposed to be a prescription painkiller that is weaker and typically less prone to abuse than many other brands. But it has now been adopted by hardcore legal-high aficionados.

5. 2C-P

This synthetic psychedelic is a close chemical cousin of 2C-B, which briefly thrived on the US club scene until it was outlawed in 2001. Users report that 2C-P – now illegal in the US and UK – causes stronger visual hallucinations and disturbing side-effects.

6. Mephedrone (Bath Salts)

Similar in structure to methamphetamine and banned by many countries. It produces a more hallucinogenic effect. In 2012, a Florida man allegedly committed an infamous act of cannibalism under its influence.

7. 6-APB (Benzo Fury)

This hit the UK club scene in 2010. It's claimed to resemble 'a mixture of Ecstasy and cocaine' but users report that it has a disturbingly jittery and speedy side-effect.

8. Salvia

Use of this legal high effectively peaked in 2010 with young users posting YouTube videos of themselves tripping after smoking it. Later that same year, pop star Miley Cyrus was said to have allegedly smoked a version of it on a music video.

9. Methoxetamine (Mexxy)

A chemical analogue of ketamine and PCP, it's classified as a dissociative anaesthetic hallucinogen. It's been sold since 2010 and found massive popularity on the European club scene. Users warn that it has very disturbing side-effects.

10. Kratom

The kratom plant is still legal in a lot of countries, including the US. It has recently become more widely available via the Internet and some users claim it is an effective painkiller but its long-term side-effects remain unknown.

The purity of a drug does not mean much unless we know potency and effect.

Dr Adam Winstock, addictions psychiatrist
at King's College London and founder of
the Global Drugs Survey

Visit www.wensleyclarkson.com to keep up with Wensley Clarkson's latest activities, including his numerous TV and documentary appearances and his many bestselling books.